ROUTLEDGE LIBRARY EDITIONS:
CHINA UNDER MAO

Volume 1

CHEN DUXIU'S LAST ARTICLES AND LETTERS, 1937–1942

CHEN DUXIU'S LAST ARTICLES AND LETTERS, 1937–1942

Edited and translated by
GREGOR BENTON

Routledge
Taylor & Francis Group

LONDON AND NEW YORK

First published in 1998 by Curzon Press

This edition first published in 2019
by Routledge
2 Park Square, Milton Park, Abingdon, Oxon OX14 4RN

and by Routledge
711 Third Avenue, New York, NY 10017

Routledge is an imprint of the Taylor & Francis Group, an informa business

© 1998 Gregor Benton

British Library Cataloguing in Publication Data
A catalogue record for this book is available from the British Library

ISBN: 978-1-138-32344-5 (Set)
ISBN: 978-0-429-43659-8 (Set) (ebk)
ISBN: 978-1-138-34318-4 (Volume 1) (hbk)
ISBN: 978-1-138-34319-1 (Volume 1) (pbk)
ISBN: 978-0-429-43929-2 (Volume 1) (ebk)

Publisher's Note
The publisher has gone to great lengths to ensure the quality of this reprint but points out that some imperfections in the original copies may be apparent.

Disclaimer
The publisher has made every effort to trace copyright holders and would welcome correspondence from those they have been unable to trace.

Chen Duxiu's Last Articles and Letters, 1937–1942

Edited and Translated by
Gregor Benton

Published under the auspices of
the International Institute of Social History, Amsterdam

CURZON

First Published in 1998
by Curzon Press
15 The Quadrant, Richmond
Surrey, TW9 1BP

© 1998 Gregor Benton

Layout and Typesetting by Aad Blok, IISH, Amsterdam
Printed and bound in Great Britain by
Biddles Ltd, Guildford and King's Lynn

British Library Cataloguing in Publication Data
A catalogue record of this book is available from the British Library

ISBN 0–7007–0618–6

Contents

Foreword *by Wang Fanxi*   ix

INTRODUCTION

Chronology   3

Editor's Introduction   11

A Note on the Texts and on Recent Studies of Chen Duxiu   31

LETTERS

Letter to Chen Qichang and Others   39

Letter to Leon Trotsky   44

Letter to Xiliu and others   50

Letter to Xiliu and others   54

Letter to Xiliu   56

Letter to Liangen   59

Letter to Xiliu   62

My Basic Views   70

Letter to Y   75

Letter to H and S   76

A Sketch of the Post–War World   78

Once Again on the World Situation   86

The Future of the Oppressed Nations   93

Letter to Y   102

APPENDICES

1 Zheng Chaolin, "Chen Duxiu Had No Wish to Rejoin
  the Chinese Communist Party on Leaving Prison"   107

2 Leon Trotsky, "Letter to Frank Glass"   114

3 Chen Duxiu, "My Feelings on the Death of Mr Cai Jiemin"   116

4 Gao Yuhan, "Oration at the Funeral of Mr [Chen] Duxiu"   121

5 Ming-yuen Wang, "The Struggle with Chen Du-hsiu"   127

6 Shuang Shan, "On Chen Duxiu's 'Last Views'"   130

7 Wang Fanxi, "Chen Duxiu, Founder of Chinese Communism"   133

8 Zheng Chaolin, "Chen Duxiu and the Trotskyists"   142

9 Xiao Ke, "Preface to the Collected Poems of Chen Duxiu"   150

Glossary   153

Index   161

List of Figures

The following photographs appear between page 94 and 95:

1 Zheng Chaolin, circa 1930

2 Chen Duxiu (left) and Peng Shuzi in 1932, at their trial in Jiangning

3 Leon Trotsky, Mexico, 1939 (photo courtesy of Alex Buchman)

4 The Provisional Central Committee of the (Trotskyist) Communist League of China, winter 1936. Clockwise from left: Wang Fanxi, Frank Glass, Hua Zhenlin (not a CC member), Han Jun, Chen Qichang, Jiang Zhendong (photo courtesy of Alex Buchman)

5 Chen Duxiu, circa 1937

6 Chen Duxiu. Chen's own penned caption reads: "Taken in the First Nanjing Prison in the spring of the 26th year of the Republic" (i.e., 1937)

7 Zheng Chaolin, circa 1985

8 Wang Fanxi, Leeds, England, 1989

A Map of China in the 1930s appears on page 2

Foreword

When Gregor Benton asked me to write a foreword to this collection of Chen Duxiu's last articles and letters to introduce their author to Western readers, I felt duty-bound to accept, as Chen's disciple, correspondent, and occasional critic. However, my great age and poor health prevent me from writing seriously about the subject. In any case, the translator has already provided a detailed introduction to Chen's life, work, and thought, his prodigious role in China's modern history, and the changing evaluation of him by succeeding generations of Chinese Communists, as well as explaining in footnotes various events and characters relevant to an understanding of the text. Moreover, the book concludes with a series of appendices that evaluate Chen's stature as a thinker and a revolutionary. As a result, there is little left for me to say. Even so, I would like to take the chance to write a few lines about the special features of Chen's life and thinking.

The first collection of Chen's writings, published in 1922 by Shanghai's Oriental Book Company, contained several dozen essays and a large number of contemporary comments and letters written by him between 1915 and 1922. In a brief preface to the collection he wrote:

> These several dozen essays are not only not works of literature but even lack a systematic exposition. They are simply a direct account of my various intuitions. However, they are all my own intuitions, and in them I forthrightly speak my mind. I parrot no one, nor do I strike sentimental poses. In that respect, they may be worth publishing. The themes covered by these several dozen essays are numerous and varied, thus demonstrating that literature is the product of social change. In that respect, too, they may be worth publishing.[1]

In just a few lines, Chen gives the reader an extremely accurate description of his literary style and his character as a man. First, he tells us that he writes straight from the heart about his intuitions, that he plagiarises no one, and that he adopts no sentimental poses. Second, he points out that literature - which should be understood not in the narrow but in the widest sense, as writing of all kinds – is the product of changes in society, so articles written by him at different times tackle different themes.

---

1. Chen Duxiu, "Zixu" ("Author's preface"), *Duxiu wencun* ("Collected writings of [Chen] Duxiu"), Wuhu: Anhui renmin chubanshe, 1987, pp. i–ii.

These two characteristics epitomise the worth of Chen's writings throughout his life, including in his last years. So the preface that Chen wrote for his "first articles and letters" serves perfectly to introduce his "last articles and letters".

More than twenty years separated Chen's early collected writings from the articles and letters collected in this present volume. In those twenty years, Chen played a leading role in Chinese affairs. At the same time, his knowledge – particularly of Marxism – and his experience progressed enormously. Even so, his essential nature – both as a thinker and as a doer – remained unchanged throughout those years. He continued to be directed by intuition, to speak straight from the heart, to avoid parroting the views of others, to refuse to strike sentimental poses, and to think and act independently.

In that respect, his attitude was the same as that of Marx, illustrated in the preface to *Das Kapital* by a line from Dante: *Segui il tuo corso, e lascia dir le genti!* (Follow your course, and let the others talk.)

This independent attitude is common to all great men and women. However, unless supplemented by another characteristic – the ability to change when confronted by something good and admirable or when the thinker's intuitions are seen to be incompatible with the real world – independence of this sort can turn into something stubborn and immutable, a reactionary posture left behind by the advances of the epoch. Many great people in all ages and cultures are susceptible to this sort of degeneration when they grow old. Chen Duxiu, however, was different. His refusal to tread that path can be attributed to the second characteristic mentioned in his preface, namely, that his writings are "the product of social change", that they change along with social thinking.

It was precisely on the grounds of this interpretation of Chen Duxiu's character that I argued in my memoirs that the views set out in Chen's *Last Articles and Letters* cannot be seen as final. Only his life was finite, not his thinking. In the new world and in the new China, Chen's ideas and his analysis would certainly have changed. Had he lived, what changes might his thinking have undergone? To answer that question would make a rather interesting study. I myself am convinced that he would have returned, on fundamentals, to the positions of Lenin and Trotsky.

Wang Fanxi, February 26, 1998

INTRODUCTION

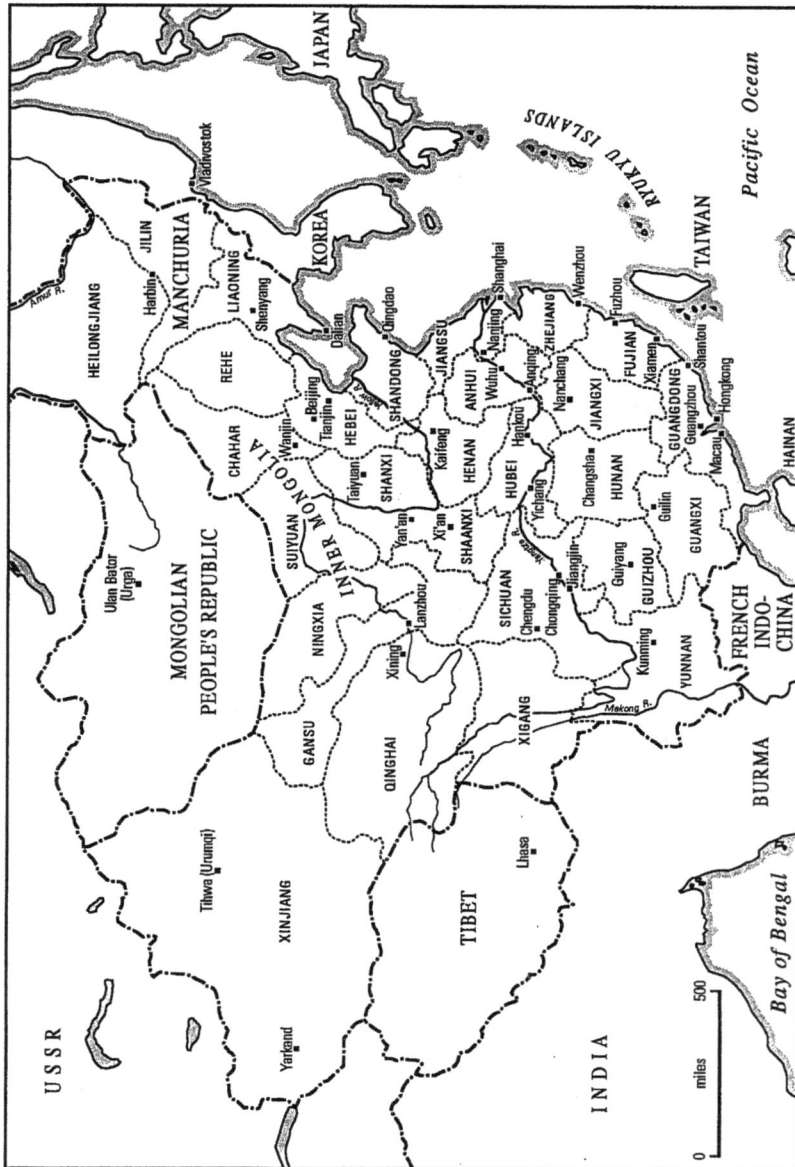

China in 1930

Chronology

China and the World	Chen Duxiu
	1879 Born on October 8 in Anqing, Anhui.
1883–1893 Conflict between China and France.	
1894–1895 War between China and Japan, concluded by the Treaty of Shimonoseki that ceded Taiwan to Japan.	
1895 Kang Youwei's reformist manifesto. Sun Yat-sen's first Republican rising, at Guangzhou, fails.	**1896** Passes the imperial examinations as a *xiucai*. At the same time, sees the corruption of the old regime and inclines toward the reformist ideas of Kang Youwei et al.
1897 Germany annexes parts of Shandong. Publication of Kang Youwei's *Confucius as a Reformer* and Yan Fu's translation of T. H. Huxley's *Evolution and Ethics*.	
1898 Britain and Russia annexe parts of Shandong. The Hundred Days of Reform end in failure. Tan Sitong and five other leading reformists are executed.	
1899 France annexes parts of Guangdong.	
1900 The Boxers occupy Beijing, attack Christian converts, and besiege the embassies. An International Expedition attacks China and enters Beijing.	

1901

The Boxer protocol includes an indemnity of 450 million taels. Li Hongzhang dies. Adam Smith's *Wealth of Nations* is translated by Yan Fu.

1901

Goes to Japan for the first time, and organises the Chinese Youth Society there.

1903

Takes part in China in the movement to resist Russia and writes for *Guomin ribao* in Shanghai. Founds the Anhui Patriotic Society.

1904–1905

Japan wins the Russo-Japanese War.

1904

Works as a journalist and educationalist in Anhui, where he founds the journal *Anhui Common Speech Journal*. Becomes a revolutionary. Joins an anarchist assassination squad in Shanghai.

1905

Sun Yat-sen founds the United League in Tokyo.

1906

Nationalist revolts in Jiangxi and Hunan are suppressed.

1907

Seven Nationalist risings are defeated.

1907

Flees Anhui with other revolutionaries. Returns to Japan.

1910

Russia and Japan divide northeast China into spheres of influence.

1911

On October 10, there is a successful Republican insurrection at Wuhan. It spreads throughout China.

1912

On January 1, Sun Yat-sen inaugurates the Republic at Nanjing; in February, he yields to Yuan Shikai, who moves the capital to Beijing. Beijing University is founded.

1912

Becomes head of the provincial secretariat of Anhui's new revolutionary government.

1913
A "Second Revolution" by Nationalists, against Yuan Shikai, fails.

1914
Yuan Shikai dissolves parliament. Japan occupies Germany's possessions in Shandong.

1915
Japan puts pressure on China with its Twenty-One Demands. Sun Yat-sen denounces the Twenty-One Demands, which Yuan Shikai accepts in modified form, and calls for Yuan's overthrow. In December, Yuan assumes the throne.

1916
Yuan Shikai dies. The warlord period starts. Cai Yuanpei is appointed Vice-Chancellor of Beijing University.

1917
Writing in *New Youth*, Hu Shi advocates literary reform.

1918
Li Dazhao publishes "Victory of Bolshevism" in *New Youth*.

1919
The Paris Peace Conference gives Japan Germany's possessions in China. *Weekly Critic* publishes the "Communist Manifesto" in Chinese. The May Fourth Movement breaks out in Beijing. The Soviets' Karakhan Declaration renounces Tsarist privileges in China. Sun Yat-sen's Revolutionary Party becomes the Guo-

1913
Leaves the government and returns to teaching. Arrested for the first time, in Wuhu. Flees to Japan after the defeat of the "Second Revolution".

1915
Founds *Youth*, to propagate science and human rights, later formulated into the famous slogan "Support Mr Science and Mr Democracy".

1916
Youth is renamed *New Youth*.

1917
Named Dean of Beijing University's School of Letters by Cai Yuanpei.

1918
Adds Hu Shi, Li Dazhao, and others to *New Youth*'s editorial board. Together with Li Dazhao, founds *Weekly Critic*.

1919
Resigns his deanship. Joins the students on the streets in the May Fourth Movement. Arrested for the second time, in Beijing. Imprisoned for three months. Becomes a Marxist.

mindang ("Nationalist Party"). The Society for the Study of Socialism is founded at Beijing University.

1920
Voitinsky meets Chen Duxiu and others to plan a Communist Party.

1920
Leaves Beijing for Shanghai. Meets Voitinsky and forms a Communist nucleus in May. In December, becomes head of Chen Jiongming's Education Department in Guangzhou.

1921
The Communist Party is founded in Shanghai, and holds its First Congress in July. Sun Yat-sen forms a Nationalist Government in Guangzhou.

1921
Returns to Shanghai and becomes General Secretary of the Communist Party. Arrested for the third time, in October, in Shanghai.

1922
Re-elected General Secretary at the Party's Second Congress. At the Party's West Lake Plenum, unsuccessfully opposes cooperating with the Guomindang. Arrested for the fourth time, in August, in Shanghai. In November, attends the Fourth Comintern Congress, in Moscow.

1923
The Soviet Union supports Sun Yat-sen.

1923
Re-elected General Secretary at the Party's Third Congress.

1924
The First United Front between Communists and Nationalists begins.

1925
On March 12, Sun Yat-sen dies in Beijing. The May Thirtieth Incident leads to a wave of strikes and demonstrations.

1925
Re-elected General Secretary at the Party's Fourth Congress. After Sun Yat-sen's death, becomes even more vocal in his opposition to Communist entry into the Guomindang. In September, launches *Guide Weekly*, which plays a big role in the Revolution of 1925-1927.

1926
In July, Chiang Kai-shek launches the Northern Expedition to overthrow warlordism and reunite the country.

1927
Shanghai workers take control of Shanghai before the arrival of the Guomindang armies. Chiang Kai-shek massacres the Communists in Shanghai and sets up a Nationalist Government in Nanjing. The Communist leader Li Dazhao is executed in Beijing. Wang Jingwei sets up another Nationalist Government in Wuhan; later, he too massacres the Communists. The two Governments unite in Nanjing under Chiang. The Communists rise unsuccessfully at Nanchang on August 1. In October, Mao Zedong retreats to Hunan's Jinggang Mountains. In December, the Guangzhou Commune is suppressed.

1928
Chiang Kai-shek organises a second expedition to the north. At the Sixth Congress of the Chinese Communist Party, in Moscow, Li Lisan takes real power from Qu Qiubai.

1929
The Communists under Mao leave Hunan and found a Soviet republic at Ruijin in southern Jiangxi. Liang Qichao dies.

1930-1934
Chiang Kai-shek launches five encirclement campaigns against the Communists.

1926
Continues to call for the Party's independence, and criticises the harmful effects on the Party of the Northern Expedition.

1927
After two unsuccessful risings by Shanghai's workers, sets up a special committee to prepare a third rising, which succeeds, on March 21-22, under Chen's direction. Leaves Shanghai after Chiang Kai-shek crushes the Communists, and goes to Wuhan, where he is re-elected as Party General Secretary at the Fifth Congress. Resigns as Party leader after again trying to end the collaboration, and finding it impossible to carry out Moscow's directives. He is then made scapegoat for the Party's defeat. His son Yannian is executed by the Nationalists.

1928
Refuses to go to Moscow, on the grounds that his ideas are too different from the Party's. His second son, Qiaonian, is executed by the Nationalists.

1929
Begins reading Trotskyist documents. Expelled from the Party on November 15.

1930
Begins to publish *Proletarian*, a Trotskyist journal. Refuses to attend a Party meeting called to review his expulsion.

1931
The Japanese invade northeast China. Wang Ming takes power from Li Lisan in the Chinese Communist Party.

1932
The Japanese attack Shanghai; the Nationalists' Nineteenth Route Army resists. In the northeast, the Japanese found the puppet state of Manchukuo.

1933
In January, the Central Committee of the Chinese Communist Party moves from Shanghai to Ruijin.

1933–1935
The Japanese advance into north China.

1934
In January, Guomindang troops defeat the separatist government set up in Fujian by the Nineteenth Route Army. In October, the beleaguered Communists are forced to abandon Ruijin and to set out on their Long March. Chiang Kai-shek launches his New Life Movement.

1935
In January, Mao Zedong is elected Chairman of the Politburo of the Communist Party. The Long March reaches northwest China and the Communists establish a base there. In Moscow, the first steps toward the Chinese Communists' Second United Front with the Nationalists are taken, as part of Stalin's new world strategy. On December 9, students in Beijing demonstrate against Japan; the movement spreads.

1931
In May, the Chinese Left Opposition holds its Unification Congress in Shanghai and makes Chen its General Secretary.

1932
Arrested by the Guomindang on October 15, for the fifth (and last) time, in Shanghai.

1933
Sentenced to thirteen years in prison.

1936
In December, when the Communists move their capital to Yan'an, Chiang Kai-shek is taken prisoner by the Nationalist Zhang Xueliang at nearby Xi'an and forced to promise to resist Japan. The writer Lu Xun and the revolutionary scholar Zhang Binglin die.

1937
The Second United Front is launched. Japan launches all-out war on China on July 7, and captures Shanghai, Nanjing, and other cities.

1937
Released from prison on August 23, after the start of the war. In September, leaves for Wuhan, where he tries to organise a democratic alliance against Japan and a military resistance. In November, Wang Ming and Kang Sheng return from Moscow. In December, at a meeting of the Party Politburo, Wang Ming starts up a smear campaign against Chen and the Chinese Trotskyists, whom he accuses of being Japanese spies.

1938
Chiang Kai-shek moves his capital first to Wuhan and then to Chongqing, in southwest China. A brief war between the Soviet Union and Japan on the border with Manchuria ends with the restoration of the status quo. Wang Jingwei defects to the Japanese.

1938
Chen defends himself against this smear campaign. On July 2, leaves Wuhan for Sichuan, where he settles in Jiangjin, some fifty miles from Chongqing.

1939
On September 3, World War Two breaks out.

1940
Wang Jingwei sets up a puppet government in Nanjing. Cai Yuanpei dies. Mao Zedong publishes *On New Democracy*.

1941

Chiang Kai-shek destroys the headquarters of the Communist New Fourth Army in south Anhui. On June 22, Germany invades the Soviet Union. On December 7, the Japanese attack the US Pacific Fleet at Pearl Harbour and on December 25 they occupy Hongkong.

1942

Japan launches a mopping-up campaign against Communist bases in north China. In February, Singapore falls; in March, Rangoon. In Yan'an, Mao Zedong lays down the Party line on literature and art.

1942

Dies on May 27 of heart disease. Has spent the previous four years under the supervision of Guomindang secret agents. Has devoted most of his time to linguistic research and to rethinking fundamental questions about the future of China and the world. His letters to some friends and a few articles, translated in this volume, were collected and published after his death.

1945

On May 7, Germany capitulates; on August 14, Japan.

Editor's Introduction

Chen Duxiu (1879–1942) is a surpassing presence in modern Chinese thought and politics. At the start of the century, he helped prepare the ground for the Revolution of 1911 that overthrew the Manchus and brought in the Republic. Between 1915 and 1919, he led the remarkable New Culture (or May Fourth) Movement that electrified Chinese student youth and laid the intellectual foundations for transforming China's politics and society. In 1921 he founded the Chinese Communist Party; he was elected General Secretary at its first five congresses. In 1929 he became a Trotskyist and in 1931 he helped found the Chinese Left Opposition, which he then led. In 1932 he was arrested (for the fifth and last time in his life[1]) and sent to prison on charges of seeking to overthrow the government and replace it with a proletarian dictatorship. Between his release from prison in 1937 and his death on May 27, 1942, he wrote the letters and articles collected in this volume.

Chen was a seminal and latitudinarian thinker, broad enough to encompass a multitude of contradictions. Some see in him the Lenin of the Chinese Revolution, but he lacked Lenin's knowledge of and gift for theory. Others view him as China's Plekhanov, because he inspired the rise of Communism in his country and served as a bridge between Marx and Mao, just as Plekhanov bridged Marx and Lenin; or as China's Lassalle, on account of his practical bent, his want of ideological polish, and his strong literary engagement. Another judgment, by Chen's biographer Lee Feigon, is that Chen was more the Moses than the Trotsky or Plekhanov of the Chinese Revolution, for after introducing his people to the new doctrines he was left behind by them when they reached the promised land.[2] But Chen's friend Hu Shi, his fellow-leader in the New Culture movement, thought of him as "an oppositionist for life" to any established authority, and it is perhaps this epithet that fits him best.

"Chen Duxiu", wrote his pupil and follower Wang Fanxi, "was best known as a revolutionary politician, but in fact he was a man of enormous versatility. He was also a poet, a writer, an educator, and a linguist. Above all, he was a

---

1. See Qiang Zhonghua et al., eds, *Chen Duxiu beibu ziliao huibian* ("A compilation of materials concerning the times when Chen Duxiu was arrested"), Henan renmin chubanshe, 1982, for a documentation of Chen's various arrests.
2. Lee Feigon, *Chen Duxiu*, p. 236. (See Note on the Texts and on Recent Studies of Chen Duxiu for the full citation.)

most audacious and independent-minded thinker. In his letter to Chen Qichang and others of November 21, 1937 [included in this volume], he said:

> I have not the slightest compunction about inclining to the left or to the right, I shall always strive to be extreme, I view with contempt the doctrine of the golden mean, I absolutely detest parrotry, I refuse to utter commonplaces that neither hurt nor itch, I want to be absolutely right and absolutely wrong in all my utterances; the last thing I want is never to say anything wrong and at the same time never to say anything right.

This unconventional and original spirit pervades all Chen's articles and letters.''[3]

❦

Although a giant of modern Chinese politics and letters and trigger of one of the twentieth century's great revolutions, for several decades after his conversion to Trotskyism Chen Duxiu's name was blackened, his achievements were concealed, and his ideas were damned by his former Party comrades, especially after they took power in 1949. Chen Duxiu in China was subjected to the same revilement as was Leon Trotsky at the hands of Stalin in the Soviet Union. Today in China, Chen's unpersoning has been largely reversed and most of the discredit heaped upon him has been removed. Young Chinese now are in a position to evaluate him more or less according to his merits; his writings have been published in new editions; friendly descriptions of his life and cause have begun to appear in the learned and popular presses. Yet in the West, Chen's name is barely known outside small circles, and the positions that he developed between 1937 and 1942 are known even less. I shall therefore preface my introduction to the writings of the late Chen with a brief look at his early political career and the context in which it happened.

The Chinese Communist Party that Chen Duxiu founded in 1921 was helped into the world by envoys of the Communist International (or Comintern) like the Russian Grigori Voitinsky and the Dutchman Henk Sneevliet (alias Maring), and owed much of its early success to Russian aid. But when in 1927 disaster overtook the young Chinese Party, that disaster was due in large part to Russian interference.

During the Revolution of 1925-1927, the Chinese Communist Party worked on Comintern instructions for national independence and unification

3. Wang Fanxi, letter, July 13, 1993.

in alliance with the Guomindang or Nationalist Party, an authoritarian political organisation populist in rhetoric but tied in practice to defending the economic interests of Chinese business groups, financial circles, and rural elites. The terms of this alliance, known as the first united front (to distinguish it from the second united front formed in 1937), were in practice disadvantageous to the Communist Party. They required its strict political subordination to the Nationalist leaders and the submersion of important sections of its membership into the Guomindang.

From the very start of this united front, Chinese Communist leaders opposed entering the Guomindang; they kept up their opposition for as long as the first united front lasted, and voiced it at regular intervals.[4] On this issue – which after 1926 became, where China was concerned, the main issue in dispute between Stalin and Trotsky – the dissenting Chinese Communist leaders were Trotskyists *avant la lettre*.

In July 1926, the Nationalist general Chiang Kai-shek launched the Northern Expedition to overthrow warlord rule in China. But first, in March, he staged a preemptive coup against his Communist "allies" in Guangzhou. Only then did he feel confident enough to send his armies north. Reorganised with Russian military and financial help and supported by a populace roused by Chinese Communist agitators, they sliced easily through the warlord ranks.

In the spring of 1927, in a second and far bloodier coup, Chiang launched a murderous assault on Chen Duxiu's Communists in Shanghai and drove them from the city. The Party's surviving forces fled to Wuhan where, against Chen's wish and on the instructions of the Russian Borodin, the alliance with the Guomindang continued, this time with its so-called "left wing" under Wang Jingwei, who had split with Chiang Kai-shek in late 1926. Communists from all over China fled to the new "revolutionary centre" in Wuhan. In mid July, however, Wang Jingwei too turned against them and killed thousands more Party members and supporters. Not long afterwards, both wings of the Guomindang reunited in Nanjing under a government effectively controlled by Chiang Kai-shek.

Around July 13, 1927, after having over a period of several years repeatedly but unsuccessfully advocated the Party's withdrawal from the Guomindang, Chen Duxiu resigned as its General Secretary.[5] He was made a scapegoat by

4. On this point, see Gregor Benton, *China's Urban Revolutionaries*. (See Note on the Texts and on Recent Studies of Chen Duxiu for the full citation.)
5. C. Martin Wilbur, *The Nationalist Revolution in China, 1923-1928*, Cambridge: Cambridge University Press, 1983, p. 144.

the Comintern for the failure of policies implemented before the summer of 1927 that he had actually (though never openly) opposed. On August 1, a fortnight after his resignation, Communist armed forces raised the banner of the Guomindang to attack a Guomindang army in Nanchang, where they briefly seized power before being routed. Even then, the Comintern instructed the Chinese Communists to remain within the Guomindang, though at the same time it told them to withdraw demonstratively from the Wuhan Government.[6] It was not until after the Communist-led risings of the autumn of 1927 that the Party finally hauled down the banner of the Guomindang.

❦

The strategy of Communist immersion in the Guomindang was not the only issue in the 1920s on which Chen Duxiu's political project differed radically from that of the Comintern's Russian leaders. The role of democracy in the revolution was another important point of difference between him and them and remained so for the rest of his life, as the contents of this volume power-fully attest. Democracy ran a poor course in the Chinese Revolution, but Chen Duxiu, having found traditional strategies for social change wanting after the degeneration of China's Republican Revolution of 1911, had fixed once for all on socialism with democracy as the appropriate remedy for his country's ills. "There are now two roads in the world," he wrote in October 1918: "one is the road of light which leads to democracy, science, and atheism; and the other, the road of darkness leading to despotism, superstition, and divine authority."[7] "Science, modern democracy, and socialism are three main inventions, precious beyond measure, of the genius of modern humankind," he repeated in September 1940, not long before his death.[8]

Chen Duxiu may have drawn his inspiration for the Party from the Bolshe-viks, but his idea of it was quite different from theirs. Like Lunacharsky, Chen believed that "revolution is the work of saints". Unlike Stalin, he opposed the creation of a strong Party chief, insisting rather that the General Secretary should be elected by and responsible to the different committee heads; he even let non-Marxists and anarchists join the Party. Under his leadership, different

6. C. Martin Wilbur and Julie Lien-ying How, *Missionaries of Revolution: Soviet Advisers and Nationalist China, 1920-1927*, Cambridge, Mass.: Harvard University Press, 1989, p. 424.
7. Quoted in Yu-Ju Chih, The Political Thought of Ch'en Tu-hsiu, PhD thesis, Indiana University, 1965, p. 68.
8. See the letter to Xiliu in this volume.

points of view vied rather freely, and though the outcome of the discussion was settled largely in Moscow, it was several years before the Chinese Party was wholly transformed along Russian lines. Even Mao Zedong, who himself presided after 1938 over a Party regimented from the centre, recognised that under Chen Duxiu the Communist movement was "rather lively" and free of dogmatism.[9] "In dealing with people and affairs within the Party, [Chen Duxiu] was comparatively reasonable," concluded the Communist Liu Ruilong.[10]

The young Chen Duxiu shared with the Chinese anarchists a libertarian suspicion of the state that partly explains his later anti-Stalinism. Other connections, too, can be made between Chen and the anarchists. Before the Revolution of 1911, when anarcho–socialist ideas were for a time highly popular among young Chinese revolutionaries, Chen's radical friends had included several anarchists and nihilists.

By 1920, Chen had emerged as one of the anarchists' sternest left–wing critics. Even so, various similarities remained between his politics and theirs. He shared with them a commitment both to radical democracy and to internationalism and an opposition to militarism, even in its "revolutionary" guise (for like the anarchist leader Li Shizeng, Chen believed that revolutions carried out by armies would simply create new forms of oppression and lead to a self-perpetuating militarist cycle). And like China's second generation of anarchists active after 1915, Chen was equally opposed to native capitalists and foreign imperialists, and put his main emphasis on the revolutionary role of urban culture and the proletariat (though not to the exclusion of the peasants).[11]

Before he became a Communist, Chen's project, as formulated by his journal *Xin qingnian* ("New Youth"), was to save China by learning from the West. Just as Europe's early Enlighteners had once looked to China for models of the rational society, so China's Enlighteners of 1919 sought their light in Western concepts of humanism, democracy, individualism, and scientific

9. Mao Zedong, "Zai Chengdu huiyishangde jianghua (1958 nian 3 yue), sanyue shiride jianghua" ("Speeches at the Chengdu conference (March 1958), speech of March 10"), in *Mao Zedong sixiang wansui* ("Long Live Mao Zedong Thought"), Reprint, Taibei: N. p., 1969, pp. 159-165, at p. 160.
10. Liu Ruilong, "Dongjin, dongjin, zai dongjin!" ("Advance east, advance east, again advance east!"), in "Mianhuai Liu Shaoqi" bianjizu, eds, *Mianhuai Liu Shaoqi* ("Commemorating Liu Shaoqi"), Beijing: Zhongyang wenxian chubanshe, 1988, pp. 129-145, at p. 134.
11. See Peter Zarrow, *Anarchism and Chinese Political Culture*, New York: Columbia University Press, 1990, for an account of Chinese anarchism.

method.[12] But they learned them in artificially compressed time, unlike the
philosophes, who had a century to prepare and spread their ideas. They assimilated an impressive list of isms, but reached real depth in none.[13] So even
democracy, though among Chen's first and last loves, was rather shallowly
rooted in his thinking, and no match for the "Bolshevisers".

❦

The "Bolshevisation" of the Chinese Communist Party was set in train by the
youthful Peng Shuzhi in 1924, after he returned to China from a period of
study in the Soviet Union. It is symptomatic of a general disregard for
democracy by many of the Party's younger activists in the 1920s that even
anti-Stalinists like Peng Shuzhi – an early Communist convert to the Left
Opposition after the defeat of the Chinese Revolution in 1927 – were not
free from "Bolshevik" contempt for it.[14] The "Bolshevisation" of the Chinese
Party was helped by Moscow's requirement that it work as a disciplined,
highly secretive faction within the Guomindang between 1924 and 1927.

But though Peng Shuzhi and his fellow-"Bolshevisers" imported authoritarian habits into the Party in the mid 1920s, it was not until after 1927, when
Chen Duxiu left the leadership, that these habits became general. The Party's
assimilation to the bureaucratic Guomindang government in Wuhan in 1927
after Borodin's political victory over Chen Duxiu did nothing to help restore
Party democracy to good health. As a result of this assimilation, observed the
Trotskyist Zheng Chaolin, "the Communist Party was no longer a closely
united party but one that was rent by conspiracies and tricks, by acts of secret
collusion, by mutual attacks, and by power struggles, just like the Guomindang
we so despised".[15]

Chen's exit from the Party speeded its drift toward bureaucratic centralism,
both because he had been the leader who most fervently espoused democracy

12. See Hung-yok Ip, "The Origins of Chinese Communism: A New Interpretation," *Modern China* 20, 1 (January 1994), pp. 34–63, for a recent discussion of the democratic concerns of China's first Communist leaders. Hung-yok Ip says on p. 52 of her article that Chen Duxiu and Li Dazhao's "cosmopolitan-internationalist commitment to democracy ... strengthened their appreciation of socialism, a doctrine which contained a marked cosmopolitan-internationalist message."
13. See Appendix 7.
14. See Gregor Benton, "Two Purged Leaders of Early Chinese Communism," *China Quarterly* 102 (1985), pp. 317-328.
15. *An Oppositionist for Life*, p. 122. (See Note on the Texts and on Recent Studies of Chen Duxiu for the full citation.)

and because the Party's rejection of him coincided with its formal resolution to ban factions and hence democratic discussion and debate. Moreover, Chen was a man of independent stature who did not need to look to Moscow for backing – something that could be said of none of the lesser leaders who succeeded him over the next few years, before power in the Party eventually fell to Mao Zedong in the late 1930s.

The "Bolshevisation" by Peng Shuzhi and his supporters around 1924 was the start of a process that took several years to finish. In the early 1930s, the Chinese Communist Party was hit by a second, more engulfing wave of "Bolshevisation" when Wang Ming took over its main leadership. The transition from Peng Shuzhi (the Party's first Moscow-educated "Bolsheviser") to Wang Ming, who received his entire political schooling in the Soviet Union and was the archetype of a Stalinist plant in the Chinese Party, reflected corresponding changes in the Comintern's role in the world Communist movement over the same period – from meddler in it to master of it.

For the time being, the series of blows that Chiang Kai-shek rained down upon the Chinese Communists in 1926 and 1927 put an end to their chance of political power. However, the Chinese Communist leaders – taking their cue from Moscow – refused (mainly for factional reasons connected with Stalin's campaign against Trotsky, who in 1926 had denounced Stalin's China policy) to recognise that the Chinese Revolution had been defeated. If they were right, then the struggle was naturally free to rise to new levels, with insurrections in the cities backed by peasant armies in the countryside. This was the course on which the Chinese Communists embarked.

Chen Duxiu and dozens of senior and veteran Communist leaders condemned this new policy as "adventurist". In 1931, after their expulsion from the official Party, these critics joined younger Trotskyists freshly returned from Moscow in a Chinese section of Trotsky's International Left Opposition. Chen's Trotskyists considered that a massive defeat had indeed been suffered in 1927 and that the Chinese Revolution was not remotely near a "new high tide". For them, the immediate task was to rebuild the shattered trade unions, re-establish the Party in the towns, and forge new links to the workers.

Central to their programme was the struggle for an all-powerful National (or Constituent) Assembly elected by universal secret ballot, since they believed that only such a strategy could bring together China's disparate economic and political struggles. Meanwhile, and until the revolution reached a new "high tide", the call for socialism, proletarian dictatorship, and Soviets should be relegated to the realm of general propaganda. The fight for a Constituent Assembly was the strategic aim that shaped the course of Chinese Trotskyism in the first nine years of its life.

Many observers were amazed when Chen Duxiu's Oppositionists espoused democracy as their platform in 1931, for Trotskyism is generally considered to be a violent and extremist variant of Communism, diametrically opposed to the idea of representative and constitutional government. But it was above all Trotsky's advocacy of the democratic slogan for China after 1927 that attracted Chen, who had started his political career as a radical democrat, to the Opposition.

As for the "dictatorship of the proletariat", Chen for a long time opposed this slogan, and when – as a Trotskyist – he eventually accepted it, he did so reluctantly, believing it to be too radical in the Chinese context, and still preferred to talk of the "democratic dictatorship of the proletariat and the poor peasantry". On the whole, Chen Duxiu and the Chinese Trotskyists stood historically for the democratic movement, unlike the leaders of the Communist Party, who – especially after 1927 – opposed democracy altogether and for several years accused the Trotskyist movement of "liquidationism" precisely because of its democratic policy.

The need for democracy not just as a central plank in its public platform but also as a main beam in the internal structure of the revolutionary party itself was another important theme in the life of Chinese Trotskyism. The official Party after 1927 was run as an elite dictatorship, modelled on the Soviet Communist Party. Until Mao's rise to power in the late 1930s, this was a Party plagued by factionalism, both self-inflicted and imported. All its leaders after 1927 used methods learned from Moscow, plus some that they invented independently, to resolve conflict and crush minority opinions. Each new candidate for leader contested Moscow's favours by tailoring his policies to suit the Kremlin; so Party politics became increasingly irresponsible and unaccountable.

In 1929, when Chen Duxiu was expelled from the Party, he reminded its leaders that "democracy is a necessary instrument for any class that seeks to win the majority to its side" and warned them that the suppression of dissident views could lead only to a regime of bureaucratic centralism.[16] But his former

---

16. Chen Duxiu, "Zhi Zhonggong zhongyang (guanyu Zhongguo geming wenti)" ("To the Central Committee of the CCP [Chinese Communist Party] (on the question of the Chinese Revolution)"), in *Chen Duxiu shuxinji* ("Chen Duxiu's letters"), ed. Shui Ru, Beijing: Xinhua chubanshe, 1987, pp. 434–454, at p. 449.

comrades dismissed as "bourgeois" the democratic, humanist, and universalist values of May Fourth for which Chen still stood, and that continued their erratic growth in the darkening circles of Chen's expelled Opposition.

✿

The Left Opposition born under Chen Duxiu in 1931 was riper and better founded than the Chinese Communist Party had been at the time of its founding ten years earlier. The revolutionaries who had come together in 1921 were for the most part political novices who had only the vaguest notion (drawn mainly from a sketchy knowledge of events in Russia) of what constituted a socialist revolution. They had been closely guided in their decisions by the foreigners Voitinsky and Sneevliet. The 1931 Opposition was quite different in character. It was born of four different organisations, most of whose members had behind them several years' first-hand experience of revolutionary activity, and the even more valuable experience of having "clearly realised their own mistakes".[17]

Chen Duxiu was a creative and independent-minded thinker, not the sort of man to toe the Party line, but a sceptic and an innovator. He had come to Marxism after a breathless rush through telescoped isms of centuries of European thought. Though his revolutionary commitment was total, his grasp of Marxism was quite shaky. Wang Fanxi has compared him in this respect to Mao:

> Both had their first love of learning in Confucianism; both built their ideological foundations in the Chinese classics; both acquired their knowledge of modern European thought, in particular Marxism-Leninism,... by building a rough superstructure of foreign style on a solid Chinese foundation at a time when they were physically as well as intellectually fully matured.[18]

Unlike some of his more doctrinaire comrades, Chen was not afraid to challenge accepted policies and beliefs, even those that bore Trotsky's personal imprimatur. The Chinese and the Russian greatly admired and appreciated one another; Trotsky even remarked that he "should learn Chinese" so as to be able to read Chen's writings.[19] But whereas for most Trotskyists in China,

17. Leon Trotsky's letter to Liu Renjing, August 22, 1930, in Shuang Shan, ed., *Tuoluociji dang'anzhong zhi Zhongguo tongzhide xin, 1929-1939* ("Letters in the Trotsky Archives to Chinese Comrades, 1929-1939"), Hongkong: N. p., 1981, p. 77.
18. Wang Fan-hsi (Wang Fanxi), *Memoirs*, p. 269. (See Note on the Texts and on Recent Studies of Chen Duxiu for the full citation.)
19. Ren Jianshu and Tang Baolin, *Chen Duxiu zhuan*, vol. 2, p. 87. (See Note on the Texts

Trotsky was a fount of pure wisdom, for Chen Duxiu – who was Trotsky's age (the two men were born in the same year) and a veteran practical revolutionary in his own right – Trotsky was an equal, whose proposals were open to scrutiny and question.

Chen believed that the essence of the greatness of revolutionaries like Lenin was their "refusal to be bound by ready-made Marxist formulae" and their "insistence on adopting new political slogans and methods of struggle to meet changing times and circumstances".[20] Chen was never prepared to accept uncritically the word of foreign Communists, for in general he had a poor opinion of them (wrote Wang Fanxi), "all the more so after Moscow had shamelessly heaped the whole of the blame for the defeat of the 1927 revolution on his shoulders". He had an even poorer view of Chinese "red compradors" who "kowtowed to foreign comrades".[21]

ざ

Between 1936 and 1938 and again in late 1939 or early 1940, Chen Duxiu and his Trotskyist comrades had a vigorous exchange of views on the issue of democracy. Sometime in 1936 Chen, then in prison under Chiang Kai-shek, smuggled an article on democracy to the Trotskyists in Shanghai, where Wang Fanxi published it in *Huohua* ("Spark"), together with his own critical comments. Three or four years later, Wang and others again discussed democracy with Chen, by then in Sichuan, in letters that they sent him from Shanghai. A selection of Chen's letters and replies, together with some articles by him from this period, forms the main content of this book.

Chen first raised in a letter of May 15, 1934, his doubts about the Trotskyist belief that the Soviet Union was a workers' state that revolutionaries must defend against bourgeois aggressors. He wrote:

> We should not just organize a new party, but also fight the illusion that the Stalin regime can be reformed. We must replace the slogan "Defend the USSR" with the slogan "Recreate the Soviet Union of October!"

This letter shows that Chen's opposition to defending the Stalinist state preceded by several years the signing of the Hitler-Stalin Pact of 1939 (after which he began to express his opposition more forcefully). It also shows that

and on Recent Studies of Chen Duxiu for the full citation.)
20. Wang Fan-hsi, *Memoirs*, p. 209.
21. Wang Fan-hsi, *Memoirs*, p. 269.

Chen did not scruple to set aside orthodox formulations of Trotskyism when he felt that they had outlived their use. But it would be wrong to represent his proposal as a complete departure from Trotskyist theory. In the letter, he made clear his continuing commitment to the Oppositionist cause and to "the movement for world revolution". "Our answer to Stalinist falsifications," he concluded, "is class struggle!"[22]

In the mid to late 1930s, the Moscow show-trials and Stalin's alliance with Hitler caused Chen to rethink even more deeply many of the basic views on democracy advanced by Lenin and by Trotsky. Chen concluded that Lenin's complete denial of the value of democracy was, at least in part, responsible for Stalin's bureaucratic crimes and that dictatorship of any sort, revolutionary or counter-revolutionary, is incompatible with democracy. Whereas in orthodox Leninist terms the dictatorship of the proletariat is simultaneously – at least for the workers – the most extensive form of democratic government, Chen no longer bothered to distinguish the various democratic rights from democracy as the bourgeois governing form, and saw "pure" democracy as an indispensable part of the socialist society. After his move to Sichuan in 1938, it seemed to his comrades in Shanghai that he had gone back in his declining years to his original attachment to this "pure" democracy: that at the end of his life he had returned to his intellectual "first love".

For Wang Fanxi and Chen's other Trotskyist correspondents, democracy was not abstract but bounded by class and time, whereas for Chen after 1937 it was a more or less transcendental concept embodied in universal institutions. Even so, Wang did not dismiss from hand Chen's formulations, and instead strove in his writings to develop along Marxist lines the elements in them that he found to be perceptive and valuable;[23] just as Trotsky continued to admire Chen, and even mentioned him as a possible member of a special committee of the Fourth International that he wished to form.[24] In their letters and articles

22. The letter from Chen Duxiu, to the International Secretariat of the Left Opposition, can be found in English translation in Stanford University's Hoover Institution under the Subject File "International Left Opposition and the Fourth International". Unfortunately, its Chinese original is not available. Wang Fanxi translated the letter back into Chinese and introduced it in "Chen Duxiu yuzhong zhi guoji zuopai fanduipai xin" ("Chen Duxiu's letter from gaol to the International Left Opposition"), *Xinmiao* (Hongkong), no. 21 (May 15, 1992), pp. 68–71. Wang points out that the original English translation, probably made by Trotskyists in Shanghai, is not necessarily literal.
23. See Appendix 6.
24. See Jean van Heijenoort, *With Trotsky in Exile: From Prinkipo to Coyoacán*, Cambridge, Mass.: Harvard University Press, 1978, p. 143. This special committee, elsewhere called the General

of this period, Chen and his Trotskyist correspondents raised – decades in advance of the mainstream of Communist dissent – issues that bear directly on the invariably vexed relationship between socialist government and democratic freedoms.

During the final years of his life, Chen wrote in the papers collected in this volume about democracy and dictatorship, war and revolution, and the future (in the light of his views on these questions) of China and the world. In these posthumous papers, Chen repeated some of the arguments that he had advanced in *Huohua* in 1936. He asserted that democracy is the content and form of each stage of human history, and must not be exclusively equated with the bourgeoisie. On the contrary, in the modern world, proletarians were the principal democrats. At the start of this new trend in his thinking, Chen simply counterposed democracy and bureaucratism, but he later ended up by counterposing democracy and proletarian dictatorship in all its forms. He completely denied the progressive import not only of proletarian dictatorship but also of Bolshevism, which he described as the twin of Fascism and the father of Stalinism. However, he rejected proletarian dictatorship not in favour of capitalism but in the name of Marxism.

At times, for example in a letter of December 23, 1941, to Zheng Xuejia, a former Trotskyist sympathiser who had later become associated with the Guomindang, he even appeared to reject Marxism itself, as irrelevant not only to China but even to Russia and Western Europe. On the whole, however, his final views are not irreconcilable with Marxism as Karl Kautsky and others understood it.[25]

In June 1940 and January 1941, the Peng Shuzhi faction of Trotskyists in Shanghai passed two resolutions in which they criticised Chen Duxiu for Plekhanov-style "opportunism" and for failing to "defend the Soviet Union's … socialist system of property" or to call for world proletarian revolution.[26] According to Peng Shuzhi, the late Chen had not only abandoned his revolutionary ideas but had lost his integrity.

Other Trotskyists, however, put a very different interpretation on Chen's later evolution, and made a far more positive appraisal of him. Wang Fanxi, for example, believed that though Chen's thinking

---

Council, was intended to be an honorary organisation; it never came into being.

25. For Chen's letter to Zheng Xuejia, see Ren Jianshu and Tang Baolin, *Chen Duxiu zhuan*, vol. 2, p. 286.

26. Ren Jianshu and Tang Baolin, *Chen Duxiu zhuan*, vol. 2, pp. 287-288.

in the final years of his life was already far from Trotskyism, ... had he lived longer, he would almost certainly have ... returned to the Trotskyist camp, since he not only had all the attributes of a genuine revolutionary but also was a shrewd and brilliant observer.[27]

According to Zheng Chaolin, at the time of the Hitler–Stalin pact Chen got angry and went too far, "but it would be wrong to take that as proof that he had broken with Trotskyism".[28] Zheng goes on to quote an article that Chen wrote on May 13, 1942, just a fortnight before his death, that in Zheng's view shows that Chen "remained a Trotskyist to his dying day". The article called on "oppressed toilers the world over" to unite against imperialism and to "replace the old world of international capitalism based on commodity deals with a new world of international socialism". The main difference between Chen and Trotsky (by then dead) was that by 1942 Chen no longer considered the Soviet Union to be a "degenerated workers' state".

❧

The Guomindang was not the sole scourge of Chen and the Chinese Trotskyists. Revolutionaries in many countries have faced state terror in the course of their revolutions, but most could find space in which to operate, either in places of lesser government control or in occasional interludes of political ferment or relaxation. But the Chinese Trotskyists faced an additional obstacle that was virtually unique to them: their new revolutionary party was equally hated both by the government and by a highly organised and influential opposition. It is probably impossible to find the same pattern anywhere else in the world save Vietnam (where after 1945 the Trotskyists, despite their relative strength, were likewise crushed).[29]

Though Chen Duxiu was prepared after 1937 to support the Guomindang against the Japanese, he remained alert to Nationalist provocations, and, despite his hostility to Stalinism, was careful to avoid assisting the Guomindang's propaganda campaign against the Chinese Communist Party. When Guomindang leaders like Hu Zongnan and Dai Li tried in 1939 to extract from

27. Wang Fan-hsi, Memoirs, p. 239.
28. See Appendix 8.
29. On the Vietnamese Trotskyists, see Ngo Van, Revolutionaries They Could Not Break: The Fight for the Fourth International in Indochina, 1930-1945, London: Index Books, 1995.

Chen views that they could use as ammunition against the Communists, Chen resolutely stuck to a position of political neutrality.[30]

In 1935 the "democratic upsurge" that Chen had been predicting ever since the late 1920s finally began in China. Yet it was not the Trotskyists (who were at first mostly still in prison) but the Communists, with their "second united front", freshly created in Moscow to chime in with Stalin's new defence and foreign-policy initiatives, who were best placed to take advantage of the new opening. "For years they had constantly misrepresented and caricatured our democratic programme," wrote Wang Fanxi, "but suddenly they took up positions identical with all the worst features of the caricatures they had made of us."[31]

The Chinese Communist Party's new turn foredoomed Chen's hopes of a revolutionary-democratic alliance in 1938, for the Communists, having occupied the space that Chen planned to enter, warned their new friends in the democratic parties against dealing with Chen Duxiu. They even branded their former leader a "national traitor" and accused him of taking money from the Japanese, just as Stalin had denounced Trotsky as a "Hitler agent".[32] But even though their attempt to turn Chen into a political pariah met with general hostility in China's democratic circles, Chen's chances of finding allies were by now quite slim, for with Stalinists and Trotskyists apparently calling for the same thing, centrist politicians naturally sided with the bigger party.

❦

The mission of the Chinese Communist Party in its infancy, shouldered in 1931 by the Chen Duxiu Opposition, was to undo the pattern of the Chinese past, which seemed to Chen to be set in an endless cycle of dynastic decay, peasant

30. Ren Jianshu and Tang Baolin, *Chen Duxiu zhuan*, vol. 2, pp. 289-290. Huang Yongsheng and Wang Yafei, "Chen Duxiu zai Jiangjinde zuihou suiyue" ("Chen Duxiu's last years at Jiangjin"), *Gemingshi ziliao* ("Materials on revolutionary history") no. 6 (1987), pp. 46-52, also describe Chen's reluctance to enter into dealings with pro-Guomindang politicians after his retreat to Jiangjin in Sichuan province in August 1938.
31. Wang Fan-hsi, *Memoirs*, p. 182.
32. For the original charge against Chen Duxiu, see Kang Sheng, "Chanchu Rikou zhentan minzu gongdide Tuoluociji feibang" ("Root out the Trotskyist criminals, who are spies for Japan and public enemies of the nation"), *Jiefang zhoukan*, nos. 29 and 30 (January 28 and February 8, 1938). This charge is now universally recognised in China as a groundless slander. See, for example, Sun Qiming, "Chen Duxiu shifou Hanjian wentide tantao" ("On whether or not Chen Duxiu was a traitor"), *Anhui daxue xuebao*, no. 2 (1980).

revolt, and renewal under a new despotic line. Chen's Communists in 1921 thought that they had found in the modern urban classes – the bourgeoisie, the proletariat, the critical intelligentsia – a way to break this vicious circle. Their unremitting commitment to this belief explains why Chen's Trotskyists insisted – save for a brief interval in 1938, under the exceptional circumstances of the Japanese invasion – on sticking to the cities, and why they never once considered forsaking them in the long term for the villages.

They were Marxists in the classic mould. True, they understood the need for agitation in the villages, but first they wanted to sink stout roots in China's metropolitan littoral, for their members were too few to dissipate across the vast Chinese countryside. Even after the Japanese invasion in 1937, Chen Duxiu stuck firmly to his belief that there could be no revolution outside urban culture. Unlike his younger comrades, he was deeply pessimistic about the chances of revolution breaking out during the war, for China's industrial base along the coast had been destroyed and unrest in the countryside could not (he believed) make a proletarian revolution. "In numbers, in material strength, and in spirit," he wrote to Trotsky on November 3, 1939, "[the workers] have gone back to where they were thirty to forty years ago."[33]

The popular view is that Mao quickly saw through the bankruptcy of an urban strategy after 1927 and turned to the villages, whereas Chen Duxiu, who did not understand the peasants, was incapable of Mao's leap in imagination. But in reality Mao arrived only gradually and empirically at his strategy of encircling the cities with the villages, after he had been forced by circumstance to move into the countryside, and for several years he continued to talk in terms of the city leading the village. Nor is it true that Chen Duxiu failed to understand the role of the peasantry in Chinese history. On the contrary, from his own point of view he understood it all too well. The Chinese Trotskyists, far from ignoring the villages as a result of intellectual stiffness or torpidity, actively resisted a turn to the countryside and insisted on striving for a new way to redeem Chinese society and the Chinese nation, rather than follow the old and fruitless one.

They failed, partly because the class of industrial workers on which they tried to fasten was too small, too little spread (in just two or three big cities), and too demoralised by defeat and terror to pay much attention to them. In a word, they were prophets before their time, for which they paid the price.

---

33. Shuang Shan, ed., *Tuoluociji dang'anzhong*, p. 77.

When the repression came, unlike the official Party they had no rural sanctuaries to which they could retreat.

Chen Duxiu had always thought, perhaps fatalistically, that the peasantry is incapable of making a modern revolution, and that only the active and widespread participation of the workers can achieve one. He was wrong in the short term, but today he and the Chinese Trotskyists would appear to have been vindicated, for the absence of democracy, legality, representation, and popular control now threaten the Party's very existence. Although the Chinese Communist Party has shown itself since 1949 to be more differentiated, flexible, and resourceful than the Trotskyists imagined at the time of the revolution, its fatal and abiding flaw is its acquired antagonism to the modern, urban constituency that gave birth to it.

❦

Chen Duxiu and the Trotskyists' legacy for China is that they upheld the standard of urban revolution and socialist democracy and pointed to a way of releasing Chinese society from the endless chain of repression, risings, and repression. Because of their democratic critique of Chinese society and Stalinist politics, they have become metaphors incarnate for a host of unresolved problems in Chinese politics.

After 1949, many of the old polemics between the official Party and the Opposition about the nature of the Chinese Revolution and the strategy and tactics to pursue in it were relegated to the history books, but one issue that had exercised Chen Duxiu and his followers in the 1930s — the relationship between socialism and democracy — became a central and burning question for young people in China, especially in the universities. The mass protests and unofficial oppositions that have flowered every few years since 1949, culminating in 1989's popular rising, are a retrospective justification of the Trotskyists' critique of Maoist politics.

The new literature on Chen Duxiu and the Trotskyists that has become available in recent years has attracted a considerable measure of attention and scrutiny in mainland China. This interest is hardly surprising, for layer after layer of the official leadership that slandered the Trotskyists in the 1930s and eventually gaoled them in 1952[34] has been discredited in the public eye and

34. On the imprisonment of the Trotskyists between 1952 and 1979, see Zheng Chaolin, "Disanci ruyu genggai" ("A brief account of my third spell in prison"), *Xinmiao* ("New Sprouts") (Hongkong), August 1993, pp. 41–47; the same article appeared, but with many deletions, in

the crisis of faith in Stalinism and Maoism is deep and general. At the same time, many younger historians have taken seriously the regime's call for truthful and factual scholarship. The new attitude among Chinese scholars toward the legacy that Chen Duxiu bequeathed his country is epitomised in the introduction by the historian Tang Baolin to a compilation, published in September 1993, of passages from Chen's works:

> Chen Duxiu changed often in the course of his life, but he stuck to certain ideas for as long as he lived, at least (for example) where the five great issues of progress (*jinhua*), democracy, science, patriotism, and socialism are concerned. Moreover, the practice of several decades has proved, and will continue to prove, that the positions that he took on these questions are essentially in accordance with the truth.[35]

In the new, more liberal climate of the 1980s and early 1990s, even Chen's Trotskyism has no longer been wholly taboo, and some scholars have begun to study it objectively. Speaking at an academic symposium held in 1981 to mark the sixtieth anniversary of the founding of the Chinese Communist Party, the veteran Communist General Xiao Ke proposed a positive assessment of Chen's leadership of the Party, and suggested that even his Trotskyist period deserved a truthful appraisal. According to Xiao Ke,

> Although it is true that Li Dazhao was a principal figure in the founding of the Party, the prime place [in that process] belonged to Chen Duxiu.... In my opinion, in the course of researching Chen Duxiu we cannot confine ourselves merely to his days in the Party or before the founding of the Party, but must also include the Trotsky-Chen liquidationist period. What were the differences between China's Trotsky-Chen liquidationist faction and foreign Trotskyists? How was their programme? What was their attitude to Chiang Kai-shek's Guomindang regime? What was their attitude to the Communist Party? What was their attitude to imperialism and in particular to Japanese imperialism? How did they acquit themselves in the gaols of the Guomindang? What was [Chen's] political attitude between his release from prison [in 1937] and his death? All these issues need to be researched.[36]

But Trotskyism remains a suspect ideology in China, and many Party officials – especially more senior ones, whose view on Trotskyism was formed by Wang Ming's 1938 campaign to discredit the Trotskyists as national

---

Hongkong's *Kaifang*. For an English translation, see *An Oppositionist for Life*, pp. 258-270.
35. Tang Baolin, ed., *Chen Duxiu yucui* ("A compilation of Chen Duxiu's utterances"), Beijing: Huaxia chubanshe, 1993, p. 17.
36. See Appendix 9.

traitors – are still deeply prejudiced against it. So younger scholars anxious to rescue Chen Duxiu the champion of "Science and Democracy" have tried to purge him of his Trotskyist commitment.

The Trotskyist Zheng Chaolin has summed up the range of suggested formulas for this decontamination: Chen Duxiu was only influenced by Trotskyism, he didn't join the Trotskyist organisation; he joined it but broke with it after his arrest in 1932; he joined it but broke with it before it became a cover for murderers and spies; he gave up his Trotskyist beliefs a few years before he died.[37] But it is impossible to stop the biography of Chen Duxiu short of his Trotskyism, so the new tolerance of and even enthusiasm for him has inevitably helped bring Chinese Trotskyism back into the public eye.

The rehabilitation of Chen Duxiu has extended even to his bones. At Chen's funeral in Jiangjin in Sichuan province in 1942, his old friend Gao Yuhan said in an oration that "Mr Duxiu is at home everywhere, and naturally an adherent of the view that 'my bones may be buried no matter where among the green mountains'".[38] Such considerations did not prevent the authorities from deciding in 1982 to repatriate Chen's physical remains to his birthplace in Anqing, Anhui province, for reburial.

Ten years later, the provincial and municipal governments designated Chen's tomb "a major tourist resource and site imbued with human and cultural meaning" and accorded it official protection.[39] By 1995, a sort of Chen-mania seemed to be sweeping Anqing, and to have infected the official guardians of Chen's remains. The local authorities announced plans to rebuild the tomb as a *lingyuan* or "garden tomb", enclosed within a park, of the sort built in the past for dead emperors or national heroes like the legendary General Yue Fei (1103-1142) of the Southern Song; or, in recent times, for martyrs of the Communist revolution. The new tomb is to be modelled on Yue Fei's; just as Yue Fei was entombed (beside Hangzhou's West Lake) with one of his sons, so Chen Duxiu is to be joined in death by his two martyred sons, Qiaonian and Yannian.[40]

In the early 1980s, a conference on Chen Duxiu scheduled to be held at Anqing was cancelled, and the journal *Chen Duxiu yanjiu* ("Chen Duxiu

37. Zheng Chaolin, "Chen Duxiu and the Trotskyists," appendix to Benton, *China's Urban Revolutionaries*, pp. 124-202, at pp. 197-199. (For the full citation, see Note on the Texts.)
38. See Appendix 4.
39. This information regarding Chen's tomb was reported in *Zhongguo qingnian bao* on October 26, 1993.
40. Zheng Chaolin, letter to Wang Fanxi.

Studies"), though announced, did not, in fact, appear.[41] In March 1989, however, a group of scholars from Beijing, Shanghai, and Anhui province (where Chen Duxiu was born) met in the capital to discuss his life and works. At the conference, and with the approval and support of the Association for Party History and its leader Zhang Jingru, a Society for Chen Duxiu Studies was founded.

A second conference was held in May 1992 in Anqing to mark the fiftieth anniversary of Chen's death. The conference decided among other things to publish a bulletin or newsletter[42] under the editorship of the historian Tang Baolin. The Third Conference on Chen Duxiu Studies was held in October 1994, in Jiangjin, Sichuan province, where Chen spent his last few years and died. This conference coincided with the 115th anniversary of Chen's birth.

The Society for Chen Duxiu Studies was declared independent, both financially and organisationally; its membership was voluntary. Though, nominally, it had some connections to the Society of Contemporary Chinese Culture, which is an official body, it was to be financed entirely on the basis of its members' contributions.

Over the next few years, the membership of the Society for Chen Duxiu Studies increased to one hundred (at the time of the third conference). The third conference elected an executive committee of fourteen members; branches were to be set up in Harbin, Changchun, Tianjin, Beijing, Shanghai, Guangzhou, Wuhu, Hefei, Anqing, Jiangjin, and Chongqing.

Forty delegates attended this third conference, at which 22 papers were presented (eighteen by their authors, four by representatives of their authors). These papers covered a wide variety of topics, ranging from Chen's views on literature, religion, women, and other subjects to his role in China's politics and revolutions.

But Chen's relationship to Trotskyism occupied the foremost place in the discussion. An article by Tang Baolin portrayed Chen's acceptance of Trotskyism as a false step, and asserted that Chen eventually corrected this mistake by quitting Trotskyism. Another article by Xie Wei described Chen's joining the Trotskyists as a logical development of Chen's thinking. Its author insisted that Chen had remained a Trotskyist right through until his death.[43]

41. Benton "Two Purged Leaders," 318-319.
42. Called *Chen Duxiu yanjiu dongtai* ("Trends in research on Chen Duxiu").
43. These paragraphs on Chen Duxiu studies in China were written by Wang Fanxi.

The students who occupied Tian'anmen Square in May and June 1989 drew their inspiration directly and explicitly from the May Fourth Movement of 1919, which Chen Duxiu led. They copied Chen's famous early slogan calling for science and democracy and echoed – consciously or unconsciously – many of his later anti-Stalinist proposals. "My biography of Chen Duxiu, founder of the Chinese Communist party, seemed especially relevant to the events of 1989," wrote the historian Lee Feigon in his analysis of the background to the Tian'anmen Square massacre.

> In the late 1920s Chen was kicked out of the party as a "Trotskyist deviationist and opportunist" for advocating many of the same ideas proposed by the students in 1989. In the 1980s some of those interested in reform looked to Chen Duxiu's ideas to demonstrate a tradition within the party for openness and democracy.[44]

But though the movement that culminated in the massacre of June 4 and some present academic trends show that Chen's legacy still lives, it set back the prospect – seriously mooted before the crisis – of a full rehabilitation of the later Chen and his Trotskyist disciples, whose return to limbo symbolises the present blockage of China's evolution toward greater freedom.

---

44. Lee Feigon, *China Rising: The Meaning of Tiananmen*, Chicago: Ivan R. Dee, 1990, p. ix.

A Note on the Texts and on Recent Studies on Chen Duxiu

In the summer of 1946, He Zhiyu took Chen Duxiu's last articles and letters from Sichuan to Shanghai. As executor of Chen's will, he edited into a pamphlet the manuscripts of a number of what he considered to be the more important letters, together with four of the articles. None of these letters, and none save the first part of one of the articles, had previously been published.

Probably in 1948,[45] those Trotskyists (in Shanghai) who remained well-disposed to Chen's memory produced a primitively printed edition of He Zhiyu's pamphlet, to which they added the title *Chen Duxiude zuihou lunwen he shuxin* ("Chen Duxiu's last articles and letters"). Today, this pamphlet is not available outside China, but it is sometimes quoted by mainland historians, so at least one copy of it must still be in existence somewhere in a Chinese library or archive.

He Zhiyu sent a copy of the pamphlet to Dr Hu Shi, who read it aboard a steamship in the Pacific Ocean in April 1949, while leaving China for exile in the United States. Hu Shi then wrote his own introduction to the articles and letters, and later sent the introduction and the pamphlet to friends of his by then in Taiwan. These people published the collection in Taibei at the Ziyou Zhongguo chubanshe ("Free China Press"), under the title *Chen Duxiu zuihou duiyu minzhu zhengzhide jianjie (lunwen he shuxin)* ("Chen Duxiu's last views on democracy (articles and letters)").[46] (There was a second printing of the Free China Press edition in Hongkong in June 1950.[47]) The Taiwan edition dropped Chen Duxiu's letter to Chen Qichang and others, his letter to Trotsky, a short note by him to He Zhiyu (addressed as Y), and one of two letters to Pu Dezhi (Xiliu).

How do we know that the original edition published by the Trotskyists in Shanghai contained these missing letters? Because Hu Shi quotes the letter to Chen Qichang in his introduction written in 1949; and because both the letter

---

45. The text published in 1950 by Free China Press in Taiwan on the basis of the original edition is dated January 28, 1948.

46. According to Richard Kagan, "The Chinese Trotskyist Movement and Ch'en Tu-hsiu: Culture, Revolution, and Polity," Unpublished PhD Dissertation, University of Pennsylvania, 1969, p. 168, the title was "changed for propaganda reasons". Kagan was unaware of He Zhiyu's role in the pamphlet's editing, which he attributed to Hu Shi.

47. This edition was acquired for me by Alex Buchman from Julia Tung at the Hoover Institution on War, Revolution, and Peace (Stanford, California).

to Chen Qichang and the other three missing items appear in recent mainland collections of Chen Duxiu's last writings (published and unpublished, including texts not selected by He Zhiyu), where their source is given as the 1948 pamphlet.

In 1967, the truncated version of the pamphlet, together with a selection of other writings by and about Chen Duxiu, was published in Taibei by Zhuanji wenxue chubanshe under the title *Shi'an zizhuan* ("Shi'an's autobiography"), the contents of which are (1) the two chapters of Chen's (i.e., Shi'an's) unfinished autobiography;[48] (2) Hu Shi's selection of Chen's letters and articles; (3) an obituary by Chen of Cai Yuanpei (retained in this present volume as Appendix 3); (4) Hu Shi's 1949 introduction; and (5) an article titled "Ji Duxiu" ("Recollections of [Chen] Duxiu") by Tao Xisheng.[49]

This English-language edition of Chen's last articles and letters is, as far as can be ascertained, based on an exact reconstruction, made from texts scattered across several sources (identified in footnotes), of the original 1948 edition.

Chen was famous for his lucid and elegant writing, but the available editions of these texts are marred by muddled constructions and unintelligible sentences many of which are probably due to poor type-setting and proof-reading. During the preparation of the writings for translation, the real or correct meaning of ambiguous sentences and misprints was, where possible, identified (principally by Wang Fanxi). The corrections are not explained in this translation; there would be little point in doing so, for each new edition has added new mistakes (though it is true that some old errors, once committed, have subsequently been copied and thus perpetuated). In any case, the reconstructed Chinese text is available to anyone who needs it. Most of the annotation to this present edition is new. Those few footnotes added (probably by He Zhiyu) to the original 1948 edition are clearly identified as such.

He Zhiyu (Ho Chih-yü), who was responsible for the original publishing of these papers, is the alias, adopted after He's release from prison in 1937, of He Zishen (Ho Tzu-shen). Born at the end of the nineteenth or the start of

48. This work, which Chen wrote in prison, was first published in 1937 in Lin Yutang's *Yuzhou feng* ("Cosmic wind"), nos. 51–53 (September–October); for an English translation, see Richard C. Kagan, "Ch'en Tu-hsiu's Unfinished Autobiography," *China Quarterly*, no. 50 (1972), pp. 295–314.

49. "Ji Duxiu" was first published in Taibei's *Zhuanji wenxue* ("Biographical literature"), vol. 5, nos. 3–4. Tao Xisheng, who studied at Beijing University, was initially close to the Communist Party, but began working for the Guomindang in July 1927. During the war against Japan he was for a time a member of the pro-Japanese Wang Jingwei faction, but he soon reverted to supporting Chiang Kai-shek.

the twentieth century, He joined the Chinese Communist Party in Beijing in the early 1920s, while a student at Beijing National University. During the Revolution of 1925–1927, he was active in his native province of Hunan, first as Party leader in Xiangtan and then as a member of the Party's Hunan Provincial Committee. After the defeat of the revolution in the autumn of 1927, he became organiser (with Mao, a fellow Hunanese, as secretary) of the Hunan Provincial Committee, and took over as secretary when Mao left Changsha to lead the armed struggle. He was a delegate to the Party's Fifth Congress and to its Sixth (Moscow) Congress. After his return to China from Russia, he became a member of the Shandong Provincial Committee, was arrested, escaped from prison, and fled to Shanghai. He became a Trotskyist in 1929, following the conversion to Trotskyism of Chen Duxiu and other old Party leaders. He was arrested as a Trotskyist by Chiang Kai-shek's political police in May 1930. Sentenced to ten years' imprisonment, he was released in August 1937, shortly after the outbreak of the Sino-Japanese War. During the war years, he worked as a middle-school teacher in Jiangjin, Sichuan province, where Chen Duxiu lived between 1938 and his death in 1942, and he acted as an intermediary between Chen and the outside world. After Chen's death, he volunteered to act as Chen's literary executor. He was arrested by the Maoist secret police in 1952 as a member of the Internationalist Workers' Party of China (representing a minority of the Chinese Trotskyist movement) and sentenced to life imprisonment. According to his prison-mate Zheng Chaolin,[50] he had collapsed in both body and spirit before he died of a stroke in prison in 1960.

By the late 1980s, research on Chen Duxiu had progressed rapidly in China: no fewer than three book-length biographical studies on Chen Duxiu or chronologies of his life were published in China between 1987 and 1989, and a major new study was published in Taiwan. All these books discuss the background to, and meaning of, Chen's last articles and letters. The three mainland biographies of Chen are Wang Guangyuan, ed., *Chen Duxiu nianpu* ("A chronology of the life of Chen Duxiu"), Chongqing: Chongqing

50. Zheng Chaolin (Cheng Ch'ao-lin) (1901–), a writer and translator, joined the Chinese Communist Party in Paris in 1922. He returned to China in 1924 to edit the Party organ *Xiangdao* ("Guide Weekly"). He was a member of the Party's Hubei Provincial Committee during the Revolution of 1925–1927, and a participant in the Emergency Conference of August 7, 1927. He became a Trotskyist in 1929, and was a founder and leader of the Chinese Trotskyist organisation. He served seven years in prison under Chiang Kai-shek. He was arrested by the Maoist secret police in 1952 and kept in prison without trial until 1979. His memoirs were published in China in 1986.

chubanshe, 1987; Tang Baolin and Lin Maosheng, *Chen Duxiu nianpu* ("A chronology of the life of Chen Duxiu"), Shanghai: Shanghai renmin chubanshe, 1988; and Ren Jianshu and Tang Baolin, *Chen Duxiu zhuan* ("A biography of Chen Duxiu"), 2 vols, Shanghai: Shanghai renmin chubanshe, 1989 (Ren wrote the first volume, subtitled *Cong xiucai dao zong shuji* ("From scholar to General Secretary"), and Tang the second, subtitled *Cong zong shuji dao fanduipai* ("From General Secretary to oppositionist")). The Taiwan study is Zheng Xuejia, *Chen Duxiu zhuan* ("A biography of Chen Duxiu"), 2 vols, Taibei: Shibao wenhua chuban qiye youxian gongsi, 1989. Later, in 1992, Thomas Kuo's book on Chen (*Ch'en Tu-hsiu (1879-1942) and the Chinese Communist Movement*, South Orange, New Jersey: Seton Hall University Press, 1975, based on his 1969 PhD thesis of the same title) was published in Chinese translation by Taibei's Lianjing chuban shiye gongsi as Guo Chengtang (Thomas Kuo), *Chen Duxiu yu Zhongguo gongchanzhuyi yundong* ("Chen Duxiu and the Chinese Communist Movement"). An early (and probably the best available) Chinese-language chronology of Chen's life is Zhi Yuru (Chih Yu-ju), *Chen Duxiu nianpu* ("A chronology of the life of Chen Duxiu"), Hongkong: Longmen shudian, 1974.

An excellent Western study is Lee Feigon, *Chen Duxiu, Founder of the Chinese Communist Party*, Princeton: Princeton University Press, 1983. For a history of Chinese Trotskyism, see Gregor Benton, *China's Urban Revolutionaries: Explorations in the History of Chinese Trotskyism, 1921-1952*, New Jersey and London: Humanities Press, 1996. (Parts of the introduction to this volume are identical with chapter 6 and one or two other sections of that study.) In August 1994, Tang Baolin, a mainland Chinese specialist on Chen Duxiu and Chinese Trotskyism working in the Institute of Modern History at the Chinese Academy of Social Sciences in Beijing, published *Zhongguo Tuopai shi (A history of Chinese Trotskyism)* in the series Zhongguo xiandaishi congshu (Contemporary Chinese history library) under the general editorship of Zhang Yufa, Taibei: Dongda tushu gongsi, August 1994. This book, though partly based on primary sources, displays many of the same flaws and shortcomings as much other mainland Chinese writing on Chen Duxiu and Trotskyism. It resorts habitually to a double standard, one – harsh and cynical – for the Trotskyists, who can do little right, and another – fawning and indulgent – for the official Party, which can do nothing wrong.[51]

---

51. For a critical review of Tang Baolin's book, see the interview with Wang Fanxi appended to my *China's Urban Revolutionaries.*

PhD dissertations that discuss Chen's intellectual and political life include Yu-Ju Chih (Zhi Yuru), The Political Thought of Ch'en Tu-hsiu, Indiana University, 1965; Richard Kagan, The Chinese Trotskyist Movement and Ch'en Tu-hsiu: Culture, Revolution, and Polity, University of Pennsylvania, 1969; and Thomas C. T. Kuo, Ch'en Tu-hsiu (1879–1942) and the Chinese Communist Movement, University of Pittsburgh, 1969.

Two of Chen's Trotskyist comrades discuss his posthumous writings in memoirs that have been published both in China and the West. These are Wang Fan-hsi (Wang Fanxi), *Memoirs of a Chinese Revolutionary*, translated and with an introduction by Gregor Benton, New York: University of Columbia Press, 1991 (a revised and enlarged edition of *Chinese Revolutionary, Memoirs, 1919-1949*, Oxford: Oxford University Press, 1980); and *An Oppositionist for Life: Memoirs of the Chinese Revolutionary Zheng Chaolin*, edited and translated by Gregor Benton, Atlantic Highlands, NJ: Humanities Press. (This book also appeared in German as Zheng Chaolin, *Siebzig Jahre Rebell: Erinnerungen eines chinesischen Oppositionellen* ["Seventy years a rebel: Memoirs of a Chinese oppositionist"], edited by Gregor Benton, Frankfurt-am-Main: ISP Verlag, 1991.) Wang's memoirs were first published in mimeographed form in Hongkong in 1957 as *Shuang Shan huiyilu* ("Shuang Shan's memoirs"); they were published in a properly printed edition in 1977 in Hongkong by Zhouji hang (Chow's Company) as Wang Fanxi, *Shuang Shan huiyilu*, and were pirated in Beijing by Xiandai shiliao biankanshe in 1981. In 1994, Shilin shudian in Hongkong published an enlarged edition of this text. Zheng Chaolin's memoirs were written in 1945, but not at the time published; sometime in 1979 or 1980, several copies of the manuscript were mimeographed under the title *Zheng Chaolin 1945 nian huiyilu* ("Zheng Chaolin's 1945 memoirs") for distribution as reference material among Party historians. In 1986 in Beijing, Xiandai shiliao biankanshe ("The association to edit and publish materials on contemporary history") published a properly printed version under the title *Zheng Chaolin huiyilu* ("Zheng Chaolin's memoirs"), with an appendix on "Chen Duxiu and the Trotskyists" written by Zheng in 1980.

This present volume would have been impossible without the advice and guidance of Wang Fanxi, a pupil, follower, and correspondent of Chen Duxiu who joined the Chinese Communist Party in 1925 and has been a leader of the Chinese Trotskyist movement ever since the late 1920s. Wang is probably the only living person besides Zheng Chaolin capable of explicating the precise meaning of Chen's last writings, which are written in a style that is frequently elliptical or arcane. Wang monitored my translation of Chen's writings, helped correct typographical errors in the various texts from which the translations were made, and clarified difficult or obscure passages and references. Where necessary, he passed on requests for information to Zheng Chaolin (in Shanghai). I am also grateful to my friend and colleague Wu Daming, who produced the Glossary, and to Aad Blok, for overseeing the production of the book.

This book uses the Hanyu Pinyin system of romanising Chinese, except in some citations (where Wang Fanxi, for example, is written as Wang Fan-hsi, which is its Wade-Giles spelling) and in the case of some historical figures (for example Chiang Kai-shek) whose names are better known in other transcriptions. In biographical footnotes, the Wade-Giles transcription of Chinese names is added in brackets if it differs from the Hanyu Pinyin transcription.

DOCUMENTS

LETTER TO CHEN QICHANG AND OTHERS[1]

Chen Duxiu wrote this letter three months after leaving prison on August 23, 1937. In prison, he had fallen out irreparably with the Trotskyist Peng Shuzhi, and his relations with other Trotskyist leaders (who had expelled him for "opportunism" in 1935) were also poor. Chen had no wish to join with these people, and indeed denounces them as Stalinists in this letter; but in 1937 and 1938 he did maintain good relations in Wuhan with a small number of his old comrades. Chen's political project in 1937 was quite the opposite of that of the Shanghai Trotskyists: they refused to engage in practical activity and confined themselves to commenting from the sidelines on the war against Japan; he believed that, for the duration of the war, the Trotskyists should put their main energy into building a united front of all democratic parties independent of the Guomindang and the Chinese Communist Party, including patriotic soldiers, on the basis of a broad programme of freedom and democracy. Chen was even prepared to cooperate with the Chinese Communists, but he was shrewd enough to see that they would only take him seriously if he represented real forces. In the event, nothing came of his attempt to foster a "democratic upsurge". Does Chen's assertion in this letter that "I no longer belong to any party" represent a definitive break with the Trotskyists? Not according to Zheng Chaolin, whose arguments are contained in Appendix 8. Chen was given to making sweeping statements and categorical assertions that in reality were often far from immutable. The question of the late Chen's Trotskyism can best be judged on the basis of the other letters and articles in this volume, which suggest an enduring interest in Trotsky's Fourth International, if not in its Chinese section.

ॐ

---

1. Source: Shui Ru, *Chen Duxiu shuxinji*, pp. 472–474. This letter is not included in the Taiwan edition of Chen's last writings published by Zhuanji wenxue chubanshe.

Dear [Luo] Shifan,[2] [Chen] Qichang,[3] and [Zhao] Ji,[4]

I have received your letters of October 14 and 17. I also received your letter of October 16 together with Monkey's[5] letter and his plan for the book (plus the letter of October 20). The book he envisages will not be easy to write. I can make no comment except to admire his perseverance in wanting to write such a book, for I am ignorant of the subject. My replying to him along these lines will dampen his ardour, but I'm afraid I can't reply in any other way. I was both pleased and concerned to hear about Shifan's marriage:[6] pleased because the news was so unexpected, and concerned because I'm not sure how he'll earn his living. [Pu] Dezhi[7] has already been here for a week, in a couple of days he'll probably be going to Hunan to be a schoolteacher. I don't want to stay here for long, nor can I do so, but I've not yet been able to fix on anywhere to go,[8] there seem to be bad people everywhere. I understand nothing about theory, and I have not the slightest compunction about inclining to the left or to the right, I shall always strive to be extreme, I view with contempt the doctrine of the golden mean,[9] I absolutely detest parrotry,

2. Luo Shifan was an old Communist who turned to Trotskyism in 1929 together with Chen Duxiu. An activist among the workers, he was at one time close to the "Conciliationists" headed by He Mengxiong. He was arrested together with Chen and sentenced to five years in gaol, but was freed early due to the outbreak of the Sino-Japanese War. He died of illness in Hunan, probably in 1939. He was arrested under the false name of Wang Zhaoqun.

3. Chen Qichang (Ch'en Ch'i-ch'ang) (1901-43), a Beijing student leader and a member of the middle-ranking cadre of the Chinese Communist Party after 1925, turned to Trotskyism in 1929, and became a leader of the Chinese Trotskyist movement. He was arrested and executed by the Japanese gendarmerie.

4. Zhao Ji (Chao Chi) (1902-1994) was a veteran Communist who participated in the Northern Expedition of 1926-1927 as a political commissar. Zhao became a Trotskyist in Moscow in 1928. He was active during the early stages of the Trotskyist movement in China.

5. The nickname of Sun Xi, whose other name was Sun Xuelu, a left-wing writer who joined the Trotskyists and at around this time was planning to write a book on economics. After the outbreak of the Sino-Japanese War in July 1937, Sun (a Sichuanese) went to Yunnan with Zhao Ji. After the Communists came to power in 1949, Sun, Zhao Ji, and Pu Dezhi (see below) were arrested and interviewed in Kunming by Zhou Enlai, who urged them to "reform"; Pu did so, and was freed immediately; Zhao and Sun stood firm, and were kept in gaol, Zhao until 1979 and Sun too probably until 1979; shortly after his release, Sun died.

6. Luo Shifan married the sister of Zhao Ji's wife shortly after Luo's release from gaol in Nanjing and his arrival in Shanghai.

7. Pu Dezhi (P'u Teh-chih) (1905-), who joined the Chinese Communist Party in 1926 and was active in literature and the theatre, became a Trotskyist in Moscow in 1928. He was arrested for the second time, together with Chen Duxiu, in 1932, and was released from prison in 1937.

8. Chen was probably worried about the Japanese military threat to Wuhan (which fell in October 1938).

9. The *Doctrine of the Mean* is one of the Four Books embodying Confucian teachings, and is

I refuse to utter commonplaces that neither hurt nor itch, I want to be absolutely right and absolutely wrong in all my utterances; the last thing I want is never to say anything wrong and at the same time never to say anything right. You're all Stalinists, you're Peng [Shuzhi]'s[10] friends, you're not my steadfast confederates. Yes, Luo Han may be a bit muddleheaded,[11] but your unbridled attack on him is a thousand times more muddleheaded. You violently denounced the Stalinists and the Guomindang, and you particularly attacked the Stalinists; though such attacks are not wrong in principle, tactically they are extremely wrong. If you carry on making such mistakes, goodness knows where you'll end up! Shifan calls other people religious fanatics, but he doesn't seem to realise that he himself has been infected by religious dogmatism! I've received Zhao Ji's letter of November 2. Although there's a slight difference of views between Shifan and Zhao Ji on the one side and Han Jun[12] and Qichang on the other, they're basically identical, i.e., they fail

commonly accepted as the work of Confucius. It enjoins restraint, tolerance, equanimity, and the pursuit of the golden mean: "Let the states of equilibrium and harmony exist in perfection, and a happy order will prevail throughout Heaven and Earth, while all things will be nourished and prosper."

10. Peng Shuzhi (P'eng Shu-chih, also written P'eng Shu-tse) (1896-1983) returned to China in 1925 from Moscow, where he had been a student leader, and joined the Central Committee of the Chinese Communist Party. He was chief editor of the Party organ during the 1925-1927 revolution. In November 1929, he was expelled together with Chen Duxiu for supporting Trotskyism. In fact, none of those addressed in this letter was a Peng supporter; both before and after the time of this letter, all were and remained Chen's friends and had not sided with Peng, though on the question of collaboration with the Guomindang during the war against Japan they disagreed with Chen. All of them were very angry about Luo Han's trip to Xi'an referred to in the following sentence.

11. Luo Han (Lo Han) (1898-1941?) was expelled from France, where he had gone to study, in 1921 and joined the Chinese Communist Party in 1922. He was active in the Guomindang army until the counterrevolutionary March 20 Incident (1926). He became a Trotskyist in 1928 in Moscow and a leader of the Left Opposition of the Chinese Communist Party. He died in Chongqing during a Japanese air-raid. Regarding the incident referred to in this letter, after Chen Duxiu's release from gaol on August 8, 1937, Chen, in Nanjing, drafted some papers on the anti-Japanese war. Luo Han, encouraged by the Communist leader Ye Jianying (1897-1986), headed off in the direction of Yan'an, the Communists' wartime capital, to discuss Chen's proposals with Mao Zedong and negotiate conditions for collaboration between the Trotskyists – Chen Duxiu in particular – and the Maoists. Before Luo could reach Yan'an, Mao contacted him indirectly in the nearby city of Xi'an to say that Chen could only work together with the Communists if he admitted his past mistakes and renounced Trotskyism. Luo thereupon gave up his attempt, which had angered Chen and was roundly criticised by the other Trotskyists. On this question, see Appendix 1.

12. Han Jun (Han Chün) (?-1945) was a leader of the younger generation of Chinese Trotskyists. He was active among Hongkong workers throughout the period of the Japanese occupation

to grasp the meaning of this war.[13] [Zheng] Chaolin goes even further,[14] but basically he's the same as you, i.e., he indiscriminately applies theories concerning the last inter-imperialist war to today, an excellent example of fitting horses' jaws to cows' heads. I still have some hopes of Qichang and Han Jun, not because their view of the present situation approaches mine but because they have a rather positive attitude to work; those who work actively among the masses might eventually wake up to reality. About cooperating with the Stalinists, my view is that there's nothing wrong with it in principle, but at present it's out of the question. To cooperate, both sides must have something to give; in addition, there must be some common activity that necessitates both sides getting in touch — yet at present such conditions do not obtain. Naturally it's crazy to talk of "cooperation"; Luo [Han] didn't mention this matter to me, you have no cause to get oversensitive about it. The rumour-mongering and vilification is clearly the work of scoundrels.[15] You're like members of religious sects: you can't see the common enemy. As for Peng and Tall Man,[16] I swear I'll never engage in any common activity with them even if they agree with me, and what's more, our fundamental views are far removed from one another. I've also received Xiang's[17] letter. And I received your letters of October 29 and November 3, together with the letter in English.[18] There's no way of doing what he suggests, nor do I want to try to

of the colony until his death in 1945.

13. The overwhelming majority of Trotskyists, Chen Qichang included, maintained a position of support for the war but criticism of its leaders.

14. Zheng Chaolin opposed support for China's war against Japan on the grounds that it was from the very beginning an integral part of the imminent world war.

15. The scoundrels in question perhaps included both the Stalinists and the Trotskyists, who were attacking one another by rumour-mongering and vilification; they may also have been those Trotskyists in Shanghai who attacked Luo Han without a full knowledge of what Luo Han had done when he tried to approach the Maoists with Chen's theses.

16. The nickname of Yin Kuan (Yin K'uan) (1897-1967), a veteran Communist who joined the Party in France. Active in the Shandong Provincial Committee, the Anhui Provincial Committee, and the Jiangsu-Zhejiang Regional Committee of the Chinese Communist Party in 1925-27, he became a Trotskyist in 1929. He was twice arrested by the Guomindang for his revolutionary activities, and was arrested by the Maoists in 1952.

17. It is not clear who Xiang was.

18. Most probably a letter from Frank Glass, alias Li Furen (Li Fu-jen) (1901-1987), who conveyed to Chen Duxiu Trotsky's advice to him to leave the country for his own safety and go to America, where he could rally support for the anti-Japanese cause. Frank Glass was a Briton who arrived in Shanghai in 1930 and worked as a journalist on various English-language newspapers in the city. Glass' last job was with the *China Weekly Review*, where he worked as an assistant editor. The nominal chief editor and publisher of the *China Weekly Review* was J.

find a way; I fear it would be a thankless task. Luo [Han]'s recent setback should serve as a lesson. What the press said was mostly at variance with the facts. I've not read the *Shenbao* interview, could you send me a copy?[19] There are too many instances of this sort, there's nothing you can do to stop them or even to rectify them. The only thing one can do is to let matters run their course, what puts my mind at ease is that I have written a large number of articles that will be material witness in the future to what I have done. Regarding the speeches and articles I made public recently here [in Wuhan], I've widely and openly made plain that they are merely my personal opinions. All I'm concerned about is my own independent thinking, I won't give up my own ideas in order to accommodate to someone else's. They're merely my personal opinion, they represent no one, I no longer belong to any party, I'm subject to no one's orders or instigation, I make my own proposals and personally take responsibility for them.[20] At present I have no idea who will be my future friends. I'm not in the least afraid of being isolated. I wish you good health.

Zhong[21]
November 21, 1937

P. Powell, who was put in a concentration camp by the Japanese after the outbreak of the Pacific War in 1941. Glass was a leader of the Chinese Trotskyist movement between 1934 and 1938.
19. Having released Chen Duxiu from prison, the Guomindang issued and published a statement saying that Chen had been released due to his "repentance", whereupon Chen sent a statement to *Shenbao* in Shanghai repudiating this claim. *Shenbao* did not dare to publish Chen's counter-statement. Perhaps the interview Chen mentions had to do with this matter.
20. According to Zheng Chaolin, Chen Duxiu's declaration after leaving gaol that he no longer belonged to any party "was mere diplomatic verbiage. At that time he wanted to unite in the war against Japan democratic personages beyond the influence of the Guomindang and the CCP, so he wanted to avoid getting entangled at the outset in the Trotskyist question;... it is clear from contemporary sources that he had by no means left the Chinese Trotskyist organization" (Zheng Chaolin, "Chen Duxiu and the Trotskyists," p. 199).
21. The first syllable of Zhongfu, one of Chen Duxiu's other names.

LETTER TO LEON TROTSKY[22]

This letter, which Hu Shi omitted from his selection of Chen's last writings, shows Chen concerned to protect the good name of Trotsky's Fourth International in China against the activities of the Chinese Trotskyist "ultra-leftists", who at the time were denouncing Chen for wanting to "put national interests above party interests" in the war against Japan, and thus for "betraying the organisation and betraying himself". Chen notes in his counterattack that the Trotskyists' passive and even negative attitude toward the war gives credence to the Communist Party's campaign to paint them as pro-Japanese traitors, a campaign of which Chen himself had been the principal victim. The letter correctly predicts that China will fail to expel the Japanese, yet it seriously underestimates the Communist Party's prospects under Mao, with his strategy of guerrilla warfare waged independently from rural bases. But though Chen believes that the Trotskyists will only grow when industry (and thus the working class) revives, he insists that abstention from activity is no option, and he urges the Trotskyists to act now, both under Japanese and Nationalist rule, in order to prepare for future political openings. The letter shows that Chen was opposed not to the Chinese Trotskyist organisation as such but to its then leaders; and not to basic Trotskyist theories but to the Chinese Trotskyists' ultra-left interpretation of them.

🙨

Before the start of agrarian China's war against industrial Japan, the Guomindang government had no intention of fighting. It was forced to resist in haste, with a woeful lack of preparation, and in some fields with a complete lack of any preparation whatsoever. Moreover, after going to war, it reverted to counterrevolutionary methods[23] to carry out the tasks of national revolution, so it is not surprising that it has suffered military defeats.

---

22. Source: Shui Ru, ed., *Chen Duxiu shuxin ji*, pp. 477–480. This letter is not included in the Free China Press edition or the Taiwan edition of the letters published in 1967 by Zhuanji wenxue chubanshe.
23. After the fall of Wuhan in October 1938, Chiang Kai-shek stepped up his campaign of political repression against Communists in Guomindang-controlled areas and his military campaign against Communist-controlled areas.

Now that first Guangzhou and then Hankou have fallen, all the country's large commercial and industrial cities are in Japanese hands. The Guomindang government has proclaimed its military defence line to be west of the Beijing–Hankou and Guangzhou–Hankou railways. Changsha and Xi'an will probably fall too.[24] If the Japanese take Changsha, they can occupy the whole of the Guangdong–Hankou line. If they take Xi'an, they will be in a position to sever communications between China and the Soviet Union. So these two cities are military targets that they are determined to capture. Although China's armies did not collapse completely as a result of the fall of Hankou, the most they could do was retreat to garrison Sichuan, Guizhou, Yunnan, and Guangxi. Economically and culturally, all those provinces are more backward than the lower reaches of the Yangtse. It will not be easy to mobilise them quickly for the counteroffensive. If Chiang Kai-shek's government is unable to get Anglo–French material aid through Yunnan,[25] there is no guarantee that even Sichuan, Yunnan, and Guizhou can be held.

China today faces three possible prospects. (1) Through Anglo–French mediation, Chiang Kai-shek recognises Japan's demands and submits. (2) Chiang Kai-shek's government retreats to garrison Sichuan, Guizhou, and Yunnan but in reality abandons the war. (3) Japan invades Yunnan; Chiang Kai-shek flees abroad.[26] If (1), then China's future circumstances will depend on the degree of submission and the Guomindang government's domestic policy. If (2), then Japan will find it hard to rule such an enormous expanse of Chinese territory; hard but not impossible, for even though the state of Japan's economy is daily worsening and Japan lacks the strength to open up China, the large amount of natural resources in stock that it gets from China, together with *matériel* and extensive new markets, will probably enable the Japanese to scrape together enough resources to support the army they require to garrison China. In addition, they have occupied some major strongpoints and communications in China with new-style weapons and defence works. So, barring big changes in Japan or internationally, China lacks the strength to drive them out.

China's newborn proletariat, after the defeat of the last revolution and the massacre brought on by the Chinese Communist Party's adventurist policies,

24. Xi'an never fell. As for Changsha, Chinese under the Guomindang General Xue Yue successfully defended the city three times against the Japanese; Changsha (and the vital Guangzhou–Hankou Railway) did not fall to the Japanese until early 1945.
25. From Burma, along the Yunnan–Burma Highway.
26. In effect, the second of Chen's three prospects was realised.

has been greatly weakened, in addition to which most factories and transport facilities throughout China have been destroyed in the present war. Numerically, materially, and spiritually, China's workers are back to where they were thirty or forty years ago.

The membership of the Chinese Communist Party is far in excess of ours,[27] but they're just armed forces with intellectuals and no working-class base at all. We have fewer than fifty people in Shanghai and Hongkong, plus probably one hundred-odd stragglers in other parts of the country.

Needless to say, we do not fool ourselves that we will grow quickly in this war, but if we had pursued more or less right policies, we would not be in our present feeble state. From the very start our group tended toward ultra-left positions.

For example, some people think that the democratic revolution in China is already over; some that the next revolution will be purely socialist in nature, with no democratic component; some that the next revolution will be socialist from the start; some that the call for a constituent assembly[28] is void of class content, and thus suspect; some that the call for a constituent assembly is a slogan for periods of reaction and peaceful movements that cannot be used for seizing state power, for which only the slogan of soviets[29] is applicable; some that the national-democratic struggle is a bourgeois task, that the proletariat can participate in the movement but should not view it as its own task, and that those comrades who propose that the Chinese proletariat should take upon its own shoulders the resolution of national-democratic tasks are

27. In May 1937, the Chinese Communist Party had 50,000 members; by July 1940, 800,000.
28. In May 1931, at their Unification Conference, the Chinese Trotskyists decided to launch a nationwide campaign for a constituent assembly, in order to "rally the revolutionary forces against the military dictatorship, and to prepare the way for a new revolutionary upsurge" (Wang Fan-hsi, *Memoirs*, p. 150). At first, some Chinese Trotskyists opposed the campaign for a constituent assembly, on the grounds that it was not sufficiently revolutionary, and called instead for the establishment of soviet power. After a short period of doubt and confusion, none of them any longer opposed the campaign. The differences among the Chinese Trotskyists in this regard concerned the role and perspective of the constituent assembly slogan and the struggle for its realisation. Liu Renjing's position was that to fight for a constituent assembly was to fight for a parliamentary perspective in China; for most Chinese Trotskyists, however, it was chiefly a strategic means of reassembling the defeated revolutionary forces and of leading them to fight against and finally overthrow the Guomindang regime through democratic struggle. At the time, only the Stalinists opposed the call for a constituent assembly.
29. Soviet power, unlike other forms of state power, is based on mass participation by the workers, peasants, and soldiers in a vast pyramid of soviets (i.e., councils) from the local to the national level. The goal of the soviet was to establish a dictatorship of the toiling over the possessing classes.

imbued with the consciousness of the left-wing of the bourgeoisie; some that, whatever the period, the incident, or the circumstances, to agree with the parties of other classes on joint action against foreign imperialists or domestic dictators is opportunism. These ultra-left tendencies have played a big part in propaganda and education within the organisation and have consequently determined its entire attitude toward the Sino-Japanese War. There is no one capable of rectifying this mistake; whoever tries to do so is denounced as an opportunist. As for the war, ultra-leftists of this sort say that they will join the resistance but at the same time they oppose rating its significance too highly. They believe that only the war against Guomindang rule is revolutionary, that the war against Japanese imperialism cannot be counted as such; some sneer at the word "patriotism", and even consider that this war is between Chiang Kai-shek and the Mikado;[30] some think that if the workers join the war, they will be acting as cannon-fodder for the bourgeoisie, and that to try to negotiate with the Communist Party or the Guomindang for joint work against Japan means degeneration and capitulation; in the eyes of the masses, the "Trotsky-ists", instead of resisting the Japanese, are filling their publications with articles bitterly denouncing the Chinese Communist Party and the Guomindang. The result is that the Stalinists' propaganda about the "Trotskyist traitors" finds an echo in all layers of the population, and even those who sympathise with us are at a loss to understand precisely who it is that the "Trotskyists" at present see as the main enemy. Ever since the start of the war, the "Trotskyists" have continued to act in this same way. Not only is it impossible for them to win support, but it's impossible for them even to approach other people; as a result, their vision grows ever narrower, even to the point where some of them have invented the theory that the fewer the social relations a member of a revolu-tionary party has, the better.

A small closed-door ultra-left organisation of this sort (with only a very few exceptions among its members) obviously stands no chance of winning new adherents; and even if it did win new members, it would be an obstacle to the further development of the Chinese Revolution.

The Stalinists failed to understand the new situation in China after the defeat of the last revolution, so they fell into many errors;[31] the changes that would

30. Here Chen is caricaturing Zheng Chaolin's position.
31. In 1927, Chiang Kai-shek launched a murderous and highly effective coup against the Chinese Communists, who had up to then been in a close alliance with the Guomindang, in accordance with directives from Stalin in Moscow. To preserve his political face, Stalin refused to admit that this defeat had happened, and launched the Chinese Communists on a new, insurrectionary

happen if the present [resistance war] were defeated would be many times more serious and give even less cause for optimism. Today, if we fail to develop a profound understanding of possible future political developments and of the real strength of the Chinese proletariat and the condition of its political party,[32] and if we fail to determine on the basis of such an understanding the proper order in which feasible policies can be implemented, we are at best garret scribblers indulging in self-advertisement and self-consolation.

After the fall of Hankou, further large-scale warfare is unlikely. The fragmentary resistance led by the Chinese Communist Party and the Guomindang in the villages and small towns will probably spread everywhere within a short period of time. In terms of modern warfare, that struggle is no more than an ebb wave, it cannot form into a centralised force capable of beating back the enemy. If the Guomindang government goes the way of the Czechs by submitting to the Japanese and ceding a large part of its territory to them, and with Anglo-American help retains several provinces in the Yangtse valley, it is quite likely under such conditions of rule that it would revert to its anti-Communist stance.[33] In that case, not only we but even the Communists would stand no chance of retaining even a semilegal status unless they reorganised and changed their party's name.

We should beware of perpetuating the illusion that we can only restart our activities after the recovery of territories now occupied by the Japanese. Even today, while Japan continues to occupy parts of our country, we should prepare forthwith to start work afresh, within the narrow space that remains open to us, though to develop our forces we must wait for a while; only when industry begins to recover, after the war (whether under foreign or Chinese rule), can our work develop relatively smoothly. When that time comes, Marxist groups, whether underground or semi-public, will inevitably crop up in a number of places; without a big movement and a central force, it will be difficult to unite them. Only a small group that, organisationally, has won the support of a large numbers of workers and, politically, has gone all out to engage in the democratic and national struggle, is qualified to be the central force that recreates a proletarian party. The initial and fundamental job of

course that led to further defeats.

32. By the "political party of the proletariat", Chen probably means the Trotskyists rather than the CCP.

33. After January 1941, the new (second) united front between Chiang Kai-shek and the Communists collapsed in all but name, and the Guomindang resorted to even more systematic repression of the Communists.

striving to form organisational links to the workers and making propaganda for the democratic and national struggle are the policies we should adopt in both Japanese-occupied and Guomindang-occupied territories, the only difference being that under the Japanese secrecy is even more essential. If the ultra-leftists who today stay aloof from the masses and the real struggle fail to realise that they were wrong to look down upon the national-democratic struggle, if they fail to change their attitude in all respects and to knuckle under to the hard work entailed in the policies I have just proposed, if they continue to brag and pretend to be big leaders, to organise leadership bodies that lack all substance, and to found petty kingdoms for themselves behind closed doors and relying on the name of the Fourth International, they will achieve nothing beyond the tarnishing of the Fourth International's prestige in China.[34]

November 3, 1938[35]

Somewhere in Sichuan.

34. Trotsky brought the Fourth International into being in September 1938, to act as the voice and spearhead of the international proletariat and to oppose the Stalinised Third International. The Chinese Trotskyists considered themselves a national section of this world body.

35. Shui Ru, *Chen Duxiu shuxin ji*, p. 480, gives the date as "X month, 1939", but this is unlikely, for Frank Glass was already in possession of this letter on January 19, 1939, when he forwarded it to Trotsky (see Appendix 2); and during the war, a letter would have needed at least one month to get from Sichuan (where Chen was) to Shanghai (where Glass was). According to *Cahiers Léon Trotsky* (Grenoble, September 1983, no. 15, p. 108), whose editor has consulted a version of Chen's letter in the archives of the Hoover Institution on War, Revolution, and Peace, it was written on November 3, 1938.

LETTER TO XILIU AND OTHERS[36]

Chen's concern in this letter is to maintain the necessary distinction between Fascism and democracy, which Trotskyists like Pu Dezhi tended to view as mere variant modes of bourgeois rule. Whereas Chen wants the Allies to defeat the Fascists, Pu was prepared to see either side defeated, in the firm expectation (based on Lenin's theories about World War One) that a workers' rising would then follow. In this regard, there was no distinction between Pu and the Chinese Communists, who in the first stages of the war condemned both sides as predators. Chen has not yet gone so far as to equate Fascism and Stalinism, and he expresses his approval of Trotsky's old slogan of "a united front of the international proletariat against Fascism".

🙊

In the past, the slogan of the Third International[37] against Fascism was not wrong. Where the Third International went wrong was in its pipedream of allying with bourgeois governments on the basis of the absurd slogan of a "popular front" and a "front against aggression" rather than organising a united front of the international proletariat against Fascism.[38] When the British and French bourgeois governments declared war on the Hitlerite state, the leaders of the Third International actually sided with Hitler while at the same time proclaiming their opposition to an imperialist war and encouraging British and

36. Source: Zhuanji wenxue zazhi she, eds, *Shi'an zizhuan* ("Autobiography of Chen Duxiu"), Taibei: Zhuanji wenxue chubanshe, 1967, pp. 63–65. Xiliu is an alias of Pu Dezhi. The "others" to whom this letter is addressed are probably the Trotskyists, including Zhao Ji, living at the time in Yunnan.
37. The Third International (or Communist International, or Comintern) was set up by Lenin and the Bolsheviks in 1919 as the "world party of revolution".
38. Between 1930 and 1933, Trotsky proposed a united front of working-class parties (Communist and Social Democrat) against Fascism, while Stalin saw the Social Democrats not as potential allies but as enemies. Subsequently, Trotsky condemned the popular (or people's) front launched by the Stalinists in 1934 as an unprincipled alliance between representatives of the proletariat and of the middle classes; this alliance, by subordinating workers to the "anti-Fascist" bourgeoisie in the capitalist countries, would hold back their revolutionary potential. The popular front, which had no precedents in the history of the labour movement, was adopted to suit the needs not of the labour movement but of Soviet foreign policy.

French workers to oppose such a war.[39] More than forty members of the French Communist Party were expelled for favouring a war against Hitler. In effect their expulsion gave succour to Hitler in his campaign to defeat Britain and France. *Xinhua ribao* ["New China Daily"],[40] which appears in Chongqing, has published numerous translations of articles by Lenin opposing the war of 1914; day after day it makes a great show of denouncing this war as a repeat performance of the last one, i.e., as a war of two imperialist states for the right to enslave their own peoples and pillage the colonies. *Dongxiang yuebao* ["Living Age"][41] followed suit, as their yesmen; on the point of this theory, I can see no difference between the Chinese Trotskyists and the Stalinists. Why was Lenin's theory about the 1914 war right?[42] Because he was not prepared to parrot the ready-made theories developed by Marx and Engels to explain the Franco-Prussian war,[43] and instead applied his own mind to observing and analysing the circumstances and special nature of the imperialist war of his day; his slogan was effective because Tsarist Russia was practically vanquished, and moreover because of Russia's huge size, so that Germany was in no position to persecute it beyond the extortions visited on Russia under

39. In August 1939, in a stunning volte-face, the Kremlin signed a pact with the German Nazis and divided up Poland with them. This pact deceived and demoralised the anti-Fascist movement and facilitated and even encouraged Hitler's conquest of Europe. Comintern manifestos of 1939 and 1940 disguised this appeasement of the Nazis by calling on Communists to take advantage of the war in order to bring about revolutions. But this seemingly orthodox Leninist line was directed not against the Nazis but against the bourgeois democrats, who (together with the Social Democrats) had by now taken over from Fascism as the main enemy in Stalin's eyes. After June 22, 1941, when Hitler invaded the Soviet Union, Stalin switched his support back to the "anti-Fascist bourgeoisie".

40. *Xinhua ribao* was the Chinese Communist Party's main newspaper during the war. Founded in Hankou on January 11, 1938, it moved to Chongqing, Chiang Kai-shek's wartime capital, in November 1938; it was closed down by the Guomindang on February 28, 1947.

41. *Dongxiang*, a monthly journal launched in July 1939, carried the English subtitle *Living Age*; Alexander Buchman, an American Trotskyist then working in Shanghai, was its nominal editor. See Wang Fan-hsi, *Memoirs*, pp. 229-230.

42. Lenin argued that war is the inevitable product of the contradictions of the world capitalist system. Practically alone among Europe's main socialist leaders, he stuck to the line of revolutionary defeatism after the outbreak of World War One, and called on the workers of each country to work for the military defeat of their own government and to turn the imperialist war into a civil war.

43. Soon after the Franco-Prussian War had broken out on July 19, 1870, Marx and Engels argued that if France (under Louis Napoleon) won, Germany and its independent workers' movement would be "*kaputt* for years". They therefore came out in support of the Germans, but on condition that the German war remained defensive. Later, Marx condemned the Prussians under Wilhelm I for turning the conflict into an offensive war.

the provisions of the Brest-Litovsk Peace Treaty;[44] thus the October Revolution was preserved. Today, we, too, rather than borrow indiscriminately from Lenin's theories about the 1914 war, should apply our own minds to observing and analysing the circumstances and special nature of this imperialist war, for all theories and slogans inhabit time and space and cannot be copied at will. Incapable of grasping the actual circumstances and special nature of a major event like the present European war, which they declare to be a mere repeat performance of past history and deal with by repeating from memory the experiences and theories of the last war, Marxists of this sort are plagiarists of the old eight-legged essay school.[45] History does not happen twice, though mistakes do. Some people have applied Lenin's theories and slogans about the 1914 war to [this] Sino-Japanese War, forgetting the special characteristics of opposition to imperialism by an oppressed people.[46] However left-wing these people may sound, in practice they can only aid Japan. Those who apply to this war Lenin's theories and slogans from past years lose sight of the special nature of anti-Fascism and can only aid Hitler, however left-wing they may sound. Though Britain and France are not oppressed nations like Prussia was [during the Franco-Prussian War], Hitler is nevertheless a Napoleon III riding roughshod over Europe rather than a Wilhelm II.[47] As a result, the parties of the proletariat in Britain and France as well as in Germany should adopt the slogan "unite in struggle against the Fascist Hitler", not "defend the motherland". Today's weapons and communications are completely different from in the past. Even if a civil war in Britain and France could be won, if it happened before the overthrow of Hitler, the fate of the new revolutionary state would under no circumstances be akin to that [of the Soviet state] after signing the Brest-Litovsk Peace Treaty! You too have written to me to say: "If Fascism wins, catastrophe will befall the human race, so we should do everything in our power to prevent its victory." You are absolutely right. But

44. In 1918 the Soviet Government was forced to accept a treaty with the Central Powers by which Russia lost the Ukraine, its Polish and Baltic territories, and Finland, places inhabited by one-third of its population. The treaty was annulled later in the year, after the Allied defeat of Germany.

45. In civil examinations in Imperial China, candidates were expected to write a literary composition in eight parts. This "eight-legged essay", rigid in form and devoid of intellectual content, became the symbol in China of stale, stereotyped writing.

46. According to the Leninist view, the national struggle of oppressed peoples against imperialism was an integral part of the overall struggle of the proletariat for liberation.

47. Actually, Wilhelm I, King of Prussia, who became emperor of all Germany on January 18, 1871.

how can we prevent the victory of Fascism? As I see it, only if Hitler loses his war against Britain and France and his defeat, like that of Napoleon the Third, provokes a national revolution, can Fascism be thwarted. To adopt a defeatist strategy in Britain and France can only facilitate catastrophe. Victory would definitely fall to Hitler, not to the governments of Britain or France, nor to the proletariats of Britain and France or to that of Germany. To equate as imperialists both sides in the conflict and to say that the workers should resist them equally is to make exactly the same mistake as equating Hitler and Brüning,[48] Nazism and social democracy. A failure to distinguish between opposites helped Hitler conquer Germany; a similar failure today may well help Hitler conquer the world. Naturally the proletariat must prepare for tomorrow, but what must it do today? Today it is already at war! In practice and in theory, there should be no ambiguity. Either support Hitler, or resist him. If you oppose Hitler, you should not at the same time overthrow his enemies. Otherwise all talk of resisting Hitler and preventing the victory of Fascism is empty. What do you think? I await your response.

March 1, 1940.

---

48. Heinrich Brüning was a centrist party leader who became German Chancellor in March 1930. Trotsky denounced Stalin for proposing Brüning's downfall at a time when the alternative was Hitler.

LETTER TO XILIU AND OTHERS[49]

In this letter, Chen defines Fascism and Stalinism as one and the same thing, and describes their overthrow as a precondition for world progress. Chen's commitment to an internationalist politics drives him to subordinate every struggle to the universal struggle between democracy and Fascism, even to the point where he is ready to condemn the Indian nationalist leaders for rocking the anti-Fascist boat.

❦

.... In my previous letter I did not exhaust the subject, so I shall elucidate my ideas further as follows. I believe two things. (1) Until this war is concluded, and even for a short while thereafter, there is no possibility of realising the mass democratic revolution. (2) German Nazism and Russian GPU[50] politics (the Italians and Japanese are mere ancillaries) are the modern inquisition. If humankind is to advance, it must first overthrow this system, which is even more barbarous than the medieval inquisition. Every struggle (including the struggle against imperialism) must take second place to this struggle. Any struggle that harms this struggle is reactionary. In light of these views, I believe that not only the anti-war movement in Britain, France, and the United States of America but also the movement for Indian independence is reactionary. Once the national struggle is divorced from the interests of the world struggle, it inevitably becomes reactionary. In reality, once India breaks away from Britain, it will inevitably come under Japanese or Russian control, and Hitler will win a decisive victory over Britain. If that's not reactionary, what is it? This opinion will not only cause Liangen[51] to gasp with amazement: you too

49. Source: Zhuanji wenxue zazhi she, eds, *Shi'an zizhuan*, pp. 63-65.
50. GPU is one of the names of the Soviet secret or political police, successor to the Cheka and forerunner of the NKVD and KGB. It was set up during the emergency years of the civil war after 1917 to direct revolutionary terror against anti-Bolshevik enemies of the revolution; in the course of the 1920s, it turned into the Stalinist dictatorship's permanent arm of repression.
51. I.e., Wang Fanxi (Wang Fan-hsi) (1907-), who joined the Party in 1925 while a student at Beijing University. He became a Trotskyist in Moscow in 1928. He returned to China in 1929 and worked for a while as an aide to Zhou Enlai. He worked as a Trotskyist with Chen Duxiu in 1930-1931, after his expulsion from the Party. He was arrested for the first time in 1931 and again in 1937. He spent most of the intervening years in gaol. He briefly worked with Chen for a second time in Wuhan in 1938. Wang was more than once Chen's opponent on

will view it cautiously, for it sharply contradicts the formulae that we learned previously. I would be most grateful if you could copy this letter to Liangen and copy my previous letter to Mr X....[52]

April 24, 1940

P.S. That the great struggle against Nazism and GPU politics is being carried out not by the common people but by Britain and France, in the form of a war against Germany, is something of which revolutionaries of the world should be ashamed. If now, by high-sounding words, we allow Nazism to win out, we should feel even more deeply ashamed and guilty.

political and theoretical questions, but on the whole he saw himself as Chen's pupil. He has lived in exile since 1949. In the 1980s, his memoirs were published in China.
52. It is not clear who is meant by Mr X.

LETTER TO XILIU[53]

*In this letter, Chen argues that bourgeois democracy is more conducive to the
emergence of socialist democracy than is Fascism or Stalinism, and that therefore
revolutionaries cannot but side with democracy against Fascism and Stalinism.
Lenin had proposed a defeatist policy for workers under capitalism everywhere, on
the grounds that defeat would trigger and permit workers' revolutions. But, says
Chen, Lenin was speaking before the birth of Fascism.*

❦

.... Regarding your views on the European war, I reply as follows. Basically
speaking, you have turned the view you previously held of democracy and
the Soviet Union on its head and inevitably fallen prisoner to current theories
and formulas, i.e., to Lenin's theories and formulas about the last war. You
have proved incapable of using your own brains to ponder these questions,
i.e., you have committed the first of the two mistakes I mentioned in my last
letter to you. Marx and Engels had never experienced the imperialism of
Lenin's day, so Lenin was unable to take over the ready-made theories that
Marx and Engels developed to deal with the Franco–Prussian War; [similarly,]
Lenin never experienced Fascism and GPU politics, so we are unable to take
over his theories about the last war. In the last world war, whoever lost, Britain
or Germany, would have made little difference to human destiny; today,
however, if Germany and Russia win, humankind will be cast for at least half
a century into an even greater darkness – only if Britain, France, and America
win and preserve bourgeois democracy will the road be open to popular
democracy. Is it possible for us to consider that the victory of Fascism is
capable of speeding the realisation of popular democracy? Your sort of
thinking is a repeat of the absurd views propagated by the "dead dogs"[54] before

53. Source: Zhang Yongtong and Liu Chuanxue, eds, *Houqide Chen Duxiu jiqi wenzhang xuanbian*
("The late Chen Duxiu and selected articles by him"), Chengdu: Sichuan renmin chubanshe,
1980, pp. 189–191. The letter as reproduced in this source bears no date and is listed as one
of three letters to "Xiliu and others"; however, it is clear from the text that it was addressed
to Xiliu alone. This letter is not included in the Free China Press edition or the Taiwan edition
of the letters published in 1967 by Zhuanji wenxue chubanshe.
54. I.e., the Stalinists. *Sigou* ("Stalinist lackeys") sounds nearly the same in Chinese as the word
for "dead dogs" (*sigou*).

Hitler's rise to power. Can we really believe today that the way to deal with Fascism is to call for revolutions in Britain and France? If we view objective conditions, there is nothing that will support such a reckless hypothesis, the sole outcome of which would be to aid Hitler and the "dead dogs". In the past, many people[55] rejected the constituent assembly and wanted only soviets. I said to them, of course soviets are better than a constituent assembly, but what's the best way of achieving soviets? Now you tell me, "We cannot forget popular democracy." But I'd like to ask you, "There's no use in simply not forgetting it, the question is, how to achieve it?" Formal and limited democracy aids the struggle for popular democracy; Fascism and GPU politics are a brake on popular democracy. From China's point of view, if Britain and France are defeated, China will have no choice but to come under the control of Japan and Russia; if Britain and France win, the Fascist movement throughout the world will collapse. Naturally, victory for Britain and France will lead to the restoration of the old East-West order, and it is easy to imagine its impact on China's domestic politics. [But] is there some better, more beautiful dream that we can dream? In the past, the Third International's slogan nationally was for a "people's front", whereas internationally it was for "peace fronts"; it rarely called for a "democratic front", and even if Communist parties in some countries had raised such a [democratic] slogan, I could not but consider it improper, for the Soviet Union itself was not democratic and the democratic countries themselves had not yet expressed their readiness to fight against Hitler in a decisive war – at that time, to raise the [slogan of a] democratic front as a gift with which to court the favours of Britain and the USA would simply be to play the role of a brake on the massive popular struggles in those democratic countries. It would have been just as wrong as the policy of rejecting the democratic front now, when all the democratic countries have already opened fire against Hitler. Supporting democracy now cannot be equated with supporting democracy in the last world war, for in those days there was no Fascist problem. I have explained this in detail above [in this letter], and the rest I explained, also in detail, in my last letter to you, you can consult it. Please send this letter to XX and the previous letter to Old X, so that I don't have to repeat myself in a new letter. You and I realised many years ago that the dead dogs are arch-criminals on a world scale (this time my opinions on these questions are not as OX[56] said, they are not emotional and

55. This is most probably a reference to those of Chen's old comrades who doubted the validity of the constituent assembly slogan before they decided to accept Trotskyism.
56. XX is probably Wang Fanxi; Old X is probably Zhao Ji. Chen usually got Pu Dezhi (Xiliu)

ill-considered), whoever overthrew such people, we would endorse. Have you forgotten so quickly what we agreed?[57] Today I say in all frankness: I will kowtow before whoever overthrows the dead dogs and Hitler, I will willingly be their slave....

to copy to Wang Fanxi Chen's letters to Pu. It is not clear who OX is; it too may be a reference to Wang Fanxi.

57. In prison, Chen Duxiu had at first shared his cell with Peng Shuzhi, but after he broke off his relations with Peng, the prison authorities gave special permission to Pu Dezhi and Luo Shifan (also prisoners) to spend two days a week in the same ward as Chen, so that these two younger men could look after their elderly comrade. In prison, Chen convinced Pu of his opinion on the question of democracy, but after his release Pu was persuaded by the views of Wang Fanxi.

LETTER TO LIANGEN[58]

Here, Chen states his theory that though over time democracy undergoes important changes, such changes are unlike those in the economic system, in that they concern not the fundamental content of democracy but only the extent of its realisation. Chen criticises Lenin and Trotsky for dismissing bourgeois democracy as a mere form of bourgeois political control and for counterposing it to proletarian democracy; and thus for paving the way not only for Stalinist dictatorship but also for the Fascists, who copied the Bolshevik example. He sketches an economic theory of Fascism in an attempt to explain the nature of its political system. Chen's defence of bourgeois democracy is not an end in itself but an intermediate stage – made necessary by the ubiquitous crosscurrent of dictatorship – in the struggle for a more extensive democracy.

❦

.... I have seen that you [and other friends in Shanghai] unanimously [disagree with my views], so in spite of my illness, I shall make a brief reply to you. The roots of your error are as follows. First, you fail (like Lenin and Trotsky) to understand the true value of bourgeois democracy. You see democracy simply as a mode of bourgeois rule, as hypocrisy, as deception. You fail to understand democracy's true content, which is: no institution apart from the courts has the right of arrest; there may be no taxation without representation; the government has no right to levy taxes unless they are agreed by parliament; opposition parties are free to organise, speak, and publish; workers have the right to strike; peasants have the right to till the land; there is freedom of thought and worship; and so on. These rights and freedoms are what the people wanted; they are the "bourgeois democracy" that people today enjoy as a result of more than seven hundred years of bloody struggle, they are what Russia, Italy, and Germany want to overthrow. The only difference between "proletarian democracy" and bourgeois democracy is in the extent of its realisation; it is not that proletarian democracy has a different content. Ever since October [1917], the vacant and abstract term "proletarian democracy" has been used as a weapon to destroy actual bourgeois democracy, and it led to the emergence of today's Soviet Union under Stalin – Italy and Germany are only following suit. Now you too are employing this hollow phrase as a

58. Source: Zhuanji wenxue zazhi she, eds, *Shi'an zizhuan*, pp. 68–71.

weapon with which to attack the bourgeois democracies of Britain and America on Hitler's behalf. Second, you fail to understand the different class functions of Fascism and of the British, US, and French imperialists. (Imperialism is the product of an alliance between the financial oligarchy and the middle classes; only up to a certain point does it tolerate the proletariat's organisation and propaganda. Fascism is the fusion of the financial oligarchy with the lumpenproletariat and the radical right-wing of the petty bourgeoisie; it wholly eradicates the proletariat's organisation and propaganda.) You fail to see that the economic system of Fascism, unlike that of British and American imperialism, rather than becoming with each passing day more and more international, has reverted to becoming more and more national, to a process of self-contained and self-supporting feudalisation; instead you think that the only difference is in the political system. Political systems are propelled by class-based economic motors, they're not born of nothing. Even if we only consider the political system as an abstraction, is the difference between the German, Italian, and Russian GPU system and the British, American, and French parliamentary system merely tiny? Third, you fail to understand the importance of "intermediate struggles". If we have our eyes only on the final battle and argue that Fascism can be destroyed forever only in the course of that last battle, that only then can the problem be resolved, then there is no point in intermediate struggles such as the anti-Fascist movement, the strike movement, the movement for the convocation of a national assembly, and so on. Instead, we can sit back and wait for the final struggle to drop from the sky. And there's a fourth point. It is an utter illusion and sheer fantasy to assume that after the defeat of Britain and France a revolution will arise to overthrow bourgeois rule everywhere. (I refer you to my letter to XX.)[59] These four errors are all founded in one general error, which can be summed up as "Closing your eyes to the actual course of historical events, blindly resorting to abstract formulae." Even the formulae of the natural sciences can sometimes be demolished: those of the social sciences are far more fragile. History does not repeat itself. To consider old prescriptions as a sort of panacea and to apply them to the complex and increasingly volatile events of today is like matching horses' jaws to cows' heads.

Since the start of the war, *Xinhua ribao* in Chongqing has made a great point on the basis of Lenin's theories about the last war of denouncing the hypocrisy of the democratic states of the British and French bourgeoisies, of opposing

---

59. XX is probably Xiliu.

inter-imperialist wars, and of labelling both sides as aggressive bandits; but between the lines, it actually sides with Hitler. I have carefully studied your letter and come to the conclusion that it is identical with what the dead dogs are saying, not merely in its ideas but in its very words and phrases. Recently I read the pamphlet *Poxiao* ["Daybreak"],[60] which is of course based on the thinking of Leon Trotsky. It goes so far as to let Fascism off completely and to concentrate its attack exclusively on Britain and America. Moreover, it defends the Soviet attack on Finland.[61] Voluntarily to make propaganda of this sort for Stalin and Hitler is surely a clear enough statement of position. Having taken such a position, how can you still claim that you are supporting neither side? If you join together the three political positions of "oppose the democratic states of Britain and America", "don't attack Fascism", and "support the Soviet Union", there is no reason why the Third International and the Fourth should not merge. So from now on, your further opposition to Stalin will simply be a contest for position between individuals; it will not involve political principle. Apart from organs of state rule such as the army, the police, and the courts, which are in Stalin's hands, is there some other Soviet Union suspended in mid-air that we can support? If there is no prospect of you changing your opinions, it is only a matter of time before you compromise with the dead dogs. And if, in accordance with your wishes (at least as expressed by the writer in *Daybreak*), the democratic states (including America) are defeated and Trotsky can no longer stay in Mexico, it is hard to see any way out for you other than coming to terms with the dead dogs!

....

July 31, 1940.

P. S. I'd like you to answer two questions:

(1) How can the revolutionary parties in Britain and France under the menace of Nazism assemble forces more easily: by employing slogans against Nazism, or by employing slogans against their own governments?

(2) If a democratic force in Germany were to start a civil war against the Nazis, would you propose overthrowing both it and the Nazis simultaneously or would you ally with the Nazis to overthrow the democrats? Or would you (like Yi Yin[62]) propose cold-shouldering both camps?

60. Published in October 1939. See Wang Fan-hsi, *Memoirs*, p. 230.
61. On November 30, 1939, Soviet troops attacked Finland. On March 6, 1940, Finland sued for peace, and admitted Soviet garrisons onto its territory.
62. A pen-name of Zheng Chaolin.

LETTER TO XILIU[63]

*This letter argues that there will be no revolutions after the war, mainly because
of the destructive effect of Stalinism on the world workers' movement and the likely
countermeasures of the bourgeoisie, which would sooner surrender power to foreign
capitalists than to domestic revolutionaries; and that a defeatist policy in the
bourgeois-democratic countries can only help the Nazis. Chen expounds at greater
length his theory of democracy, which – he explains – cannot be reduced to the
mere existence of a parliament; indeed, the history of humankind can be viewed
as the history – still in progress – of democratisation, whose ultimate product will
be not the class-based democracy of the bourgeoisie but mass democracy, i.e., full
democracy, a concept apparently coterminous for Chen with proletarian democracy.
The Bolsheviks' failure to understand and appreciate the rich content of democracy
has led them to slight democracy and even to reject it root and branch. Their
attitude led ultimately to Stalin, who is a product, not the initiator, of the Stalinist
system. Chen goes on to reject the orthodox Trotskyist view of the Soviet Union
as a workers' state, albeit degenerated and bureaucratised, that revolutionaries must
support against the bourgeois states. (Chen had first questioned in a letter dated
May 15, 1934, to the International Secretariat of the Left Opposition the theory
that the Soviet Union was a workers' state.[64]) Stalin, Hitler, and Mussolini are
the three main bulwarks of reaction, to the destruction of which all efforts should
be bent. And the best prospect for proletarian revolution lies in the defeat of
Germany, though even there liberal forces will rise before socialist ones.*

❦

Dear Xiliu,

I enclosed with yesterday's letter a letter from [Zheng] Chaolin; I trust you've
already received it. I received your letter of July 21 and that of Shouyi,[65] and
I have read them both, but ill health prevented me from replying to them, and
still does. (It took me more than twenty days to finish the present letter; as you

63. Source: Zhuanji wenxue zazhi she, eds, *Shi'an zizhuan*, pp. 72-81.
64. See Chen's letter of May 15, 1934, to the International Secretariat, kept in Stanford
University's Hoover Institution under the Subject File "International Left Opposition and the
Fourth International".
65. A pen-name of Wang Fanxi.

can imagine, I'm not in the best of spirits.) Please don't misinterpret my failure to reply.

Your letter says: "His [Shouyi's] understanding of democracy and his view of the world situation is too optimistic, I'm afraid he's somewhat naive." Our discussion revolves precisely around the following two questions. (1) After the war, will there be a revolution in the defeated countries? (2) Should we support democracy? You call him naive (actually, it's reactionary) on the one hand and still claim that he's right on the other. Do you yourself realise that your position is self-contradictory?

Regarding the first question, all I can do is answer no, especially where Britain and America are concerned. On this point, [He] Zishen and Xizhi[66] have insisted even more vigorously than I that there will be no revolutionary situation in Britain and France, and for the following reasons. (1) The revolutionary forces in these countries have already been eradicated by Stalin. (2) The bourgeoisie in these countries has experienced [the revolutions of] 1871 and 1917; so in the event of defeat, they would sooner hand over their weapons to the foreign enemy than allow an internal enemy to profit from them. (3) Germany's armaments, military tactics, and methods of rule in the occupied territories are different from those used in 1871 [in the Franco-Prussian War] and in 1917. If the British and French governments fall,[67] for a while there is no possibility of sudden mutinies. (4) Germany has not yet achieved world hegemony; once Germany is defeated, the war will be over. If the Nazis fall, they are unlikely to be succeeded by another Fascist state. (The situation in Britain and France would be quite different.) When the time comes, the Social Democratic Party and the other liberal parties can raise their heads again; although such a turn could only benefit the emergence of a revolutionary movement, one could hardly say that Hitler's downfall would lead immediately to a revolution in Germany, since there is no revolutionary party there. For these reasons, our old formula about "revolutions breaking out in the defeated countries in the wake of an imperialist war" has been invalidated. Only those who cling to shibboleths and close their eyes to the course of history can dream of 1917 and claim that this war is a repeat performance of the last one. Since there is no prospect of revolution in Britain or France, what (other than helping Hitler win the war) is the point of adopting

---

66. The pseudonym of Wu Jiyan (Wu Chi-yen) (1898–1940), a returned student from Moscow and nephew of Chen Duxiu. Wu became a Trotskyist in 1929.
67. The French government had already fallen by this time.

a defeatist position in those countries? History does not repeat itself, but human error does. We used to think that the Brüning cabinet and Hitler were identical, and in so doing we helped the Nazis into power; today we equate German Nazism and British and French democracy and have helped Hitler to subdue France, with its democratic traditions. I can argue further that if people continue to despise democracy and worship dictatorship, then, as Shouyi says, "Regardless of good and bad, humankind can choose only between Fascist dictatorship and socialist dictatorship." In other words, the only choice is between the political system of Russia and that of Germany: which means that even if the defeat of Britain and France provoked a revolution, it would, like a victory for Hitler, have the effect only of plunging the world even deeper into darkness and degeneracy. One GPU-style Soviet Russia is enough to stifle people: could you endure a whole series of new GPU states in France, America, and Britain? So we had better have a considered debate about the second question, which is (as Shouyi put it): "The main difference between us concerns democracy."

Regarding this second question, for the last six or seven years I have deeply pondered the experience of Soviet Russia over the last two decades before arriving at my present views. (1) Without a state in which the broad masses of the people participate there can be no broad democracy: in the absence of broad democracy, so-called popular state power or proletarian dictatorship will inevitably drift toward a Stalin-style GPU system controlled by a tiny minority of people. Such a system is the necessary outcome of such a situation; it is not because Stalin is particularly vicious. (2) To replace bourgeois democracy with a state in which the broad masses of the people participate is to go forward; to replace British, French, or American democracy with German or Russian dictatorship is to go backward. Those who (directly or indirectly, knowingly or unknowingly) assist in a retrogression are reactionary, however left-wing they may sound. (3) Democracy is not merely an abstract term: it has a specific content. The content of proletarian democracy is broadly similar to that of bourgeois democracy; the only difference is that it is broader in the scope of its implementation. (See my previous letter and the diagram in the latter part of this letter.) (4) Though the content of democracy includes the parliamentary system, such a system does not exhaust democracy's content. Many people have for years equated democracy with a parliamentary system, and in rejecting the one have also rejected the other; precisely this is the chief cause of the degeneration of Soviet Russia. Parliamentarism can expire, it can become a relic of the past, but the same is not true of democracy; a soviet system without democratic content remains a representative system that is democratic in form only or even resembles the soviets in Russia; it will be inferior even to bourgeois formal democracy. (5) Democracy is the standard beneath which the oppressed peoples of every age – in ancient Greece and Rome, now and tomorrow – resist the minority privileged class, it is not merely an historical phenomenon bound to a particular age, a mere form of bourgeois rule belonging to a period now past. If democratism is already past its time, gone never to return, then politics and the state too are already past their time, already dead and buried. To say that democracy is but a form of bourgeois rule while the sole form of proletarian state power is dictatorship and can under no circumstances be democratic is to justify Stalin's crimes and to render superfluous Lenin's description of democracy as "an antitoxin to bureaucracy". Leon Trotsky's call to struggle for the restoration of democracy in the soviets, the trade unions, and the party also becomes a cry for the return of the past, a call for common people to shed blood for ghosts. To say that proletarian democracy and bourgeois democracy are different is to fail to grasp democracy's basic content (habeus corpus, the open existence of an opposition, freedom of thought and of the press, the right to strike and to vote, etc.), which is the same whether it be proletarian or bourgeois. To say that there is no relationship between Stalin's crimes and the system of proletarian dictatorship is tantamount to saying that those crimes are not the product of violations committed ever since October (these violations of democracy did not start with Stalin) against the basic content of democracy by the Soviet Union, but are the product instead of Stalin's viciousness – a wholly idealist explanation. Stalin's crimes are a logical development of proletarian dictatorship. Are they not also the product of the power that has accrued since October to the secret police, and of a whole series of anti-democratic dictatorships that forbid parties, factions, freedom of thought and of the press, and freedom to strike and vote? Unless such democratic freedoms are restored, anyone who succeeds Stalin could become "grand dictator". So to ascribe to Stalin all the Soviet Union's evils rather than trace their source to the harmful nature of the Soviet dictatorship is tantamount to saying that by toppling Stalin all the Soviet Union's wrongs would be righted. Such prejudices, which fetishise the individual and neglect the system, are unworthy of any fair-minded politician. The experience of the Soviet Union over the last twenty and particularly the last ten years should cause us to reflect. If we fail to trace the origin of such defects to the system and to draw the appropriate lessons, if we simply screw up our eyes and oppose Stalin, we will never see the truth. With one Stalin gone, innumerable other Stalins will spring to life in Russia and other countries. In Soviet Russia after October, it was clearly the dictatorship that produced Stalin rather than the other way round. If we take the position that bourgeois democracy has already reached the point at which its social momentum is spent, that there is no longer any need to struggle for democracy, then we are saying that the proletarian state has no need for democracy, a point of view that spells ruin for all times! (6) The content of modern democracy is far richer than that of democracy in ancient Greece and Rome, its reach far wider. Because the modern age is the age of bourgeois rule, we call this democracy bourgeois. In reality, however, this system is not wholly welcome to the bourgeoisie, but is the accomplishment of the tens of millions of common people who over the last five to six hundred years have spilt their blood in struggle. Science, modern democracy, and socialism are three main inventions, precious beyond measure, of the genius of modern humankind; unfortunately, since the October Revolution democracy has been rejected together with bourgeois rule; dictatorship has been substituted for democracy, the basic content of democracy has been repudiated, and so-called "proletarian democracy" or "mass democracy" is nothing more than verbiage void of all real content, false colours under which to resist bourgeois democracy. Having seized state power, the proletariat will have at its disposal large-scale nationalised industry, armed forces, police, courts, and a soviet electoral law. With such useful weapons to hand, it will be strong enough to suppress bourgeois counterrevolution and will have no need to substitute dictatorship for democracy. Dictatorship is just a sharp knife, what it today does to its enemies it will tomorrow do to itself. Lenin in his time was aware that democracy is "an antitoxin to bureaucracy" but did not conscientiously apply democratic norms, for example by abolishing the secret police, tolerating the open existence of opposition parties, and allowing people to think, publish, strike, and vote freely. Leon Trotsky only discovered after personally experiencing the dictator's knife that the party, the trade unions, and the soviets at all levels need democracy and free elections, but by then it was too late! The rest of the Bolsheviks, more ignorant, lauded dictatorship even more highly and cursed democracy as worse than dogshit. This preposterous idea swept the world in the wake of the authority of the October Revolution. Mussolini was the first to apply it and next came Hitler, while in the land of its birth –

the Soviet Union – the dictatorship was intensified and all manner of crimes were committed, whereupon the hangers-on and their spawn of the cult of dictatorship spread across the entire planet, particularly in Europe, so that today three of the five powers are dictatorships. (So it's untrue that the East needs democracy whereas the West doesn't.) The first is Moscow, the second is Berlin, and the third is Rome.[68] These three bulwarks of reaction have turned the present into a new middle ages, and they now plan to turn thinking humans into unthinking mechanical beasts of burden who jump to the dictators' whip; if humankind is powerless to overthrow these three bulwarks of reaction, its fate is clear. So today all struggles throughout the world will have meaning only if they unite to overthrow these three bulwarks of reaction; otherwise, whatever sonorous names they may go under (proletarian revolution, national revolution), from an objective point of view they will unwittingly help to consolidate and extend the power of the three bulwarks. If we recognise that the overthrow of these bulwarks is the main objective, first we must concede that even the imperfect democracy of Britain, France, and America is worth defending; second, we must repudiate the bankrupt theory of Liu Renjing,[69] which holds that whatever the time and whatever the event, the proletariat cannot act jointly with other classes. This theory clearly could not be applied at the time of [Chiang Kai-shek's] Northern Expedition [of 1926-1927], nor can it be applied in the War of Resistance against Japan or in today's world war; if applied, it could only play a reactionary role. [Chen Qi]chang says: "Today, in the midst of war, the obvious distinction between democracy and Fascism has been lost, or is about to be lost." I find this sentence really baffling! (1) From the point of view of the political system, the absolute distinction between democracy and Fascism will persist forever. (2) If the author means by this statement that democracy in Britain, France, and America is turning more and more into Fascism, then even if that opinion were true, it would be absolutely wrong to take it as a reason to welcome dictatorship and oppose democracy. (3) If Britain, France, and America go Fascist, it will be partly because the Third International and the Fourth

68. Chen forgot to name Japan among the dictatorships.
69. Liu Renjing (Liu Jen-ching) (1902-1987), a founding member of the Chinese Communist Party and General Secretary of the Socialist League of Youth, joined the Left Opposition in Moscow and visited Trotsky in Prinkipo, Turkey, in 1929. After returning to China, he played a part in organising the first groups of Chinese Trotskyists, and helped Harold Isaacs write his book *The Tragedy of the Chinese Revolution*. He was arrested in 1934, and recanted in prison. After 1949, he recanted again, this time to the Maoists. He died in a car accident in 1987.

International helped Hitler achieve complete victory: Hitler's army will bring Fascism to whichever territories it conquers; but for that army, the democratic traditions of Britain, France, and America could not so easily be crushed. To equate the wartime strengthening of the cabinet with going Fascist is to fail to understand the first thing about Fascism. (4) I would ask those people who believe that the distinction between the democratic countries and Fascism has already been lost to open their eyes and look at this table of comparisons.

   (i)   Democracy in Britain, America, and Pre-War France.
   (ii) Fascism in Russia, Germany, and Italy. (The political system of Soviet Russia was the model for Germany and Italy, so these three countries can be classified together.)

A (i)   Parliamentary elections are contested by all parties (including opposition parties). Though each constituency is monopolised by a [particular] party, each party must publish an election programme and make election addresses in order to cater to the people's demands, for the electorate is, through suffrage, the final arbiter. Meetings are attended by lively discussion and debate.

A (ii) Elections to the soviets or to the national assembly are fixed by the government party. These bodies meet simply to raise their hands in assent, not to debate.

B (i)   No one may be deprived of liberty or life without first being brought before a court.

B (ii) The secret police may arrest and kill people at will.

C (i)   Opposition parties, even the Communist Party, are openly permitted.

C (ii) The one-party state permits the existence of no other party.

D (i)   People are more or less free to think, say, and publish what they want.

D (ii) There is an absolute prohibition on freedom of thought, speech, and the press.

E (i)   To strike is not in itself a crime.

E (ii) Strikes are outlawed, i.e., criminal.

Judging from this table, tell me when in Britain and America the distinction between the two systems was lost? And as for France, why was it lost? What Communist, having studied this table, is still prepared to condemn bourgeois democracy? Surely the age of religious superstition is of the past and it is time we came to our senses! If, in the future, revolutionaries continue to believe that "democracy belongs to the past; proletarian state power can take the form only of a dictatorship, never that of a democracy", they will merely allow the GPU to trample underfoot the whole of humankind; moreover, since such a revolution cannot break out after the defeat of Britain and France, in whose ultimate interest is your proposal to adopt a defeatist slogan in those countries? Stalin's first ingenious move was to replace the slogan against Fascism with one against imperialism; his second step was to launch a sneak attack on Britain, France, and America in order to defend Fascism. You are going the same way: your second step is quite clear from *Daybreak* and from Shouyi's letter to me! Shouyi and his friends' attitude toward the world war is based on their view of the nature of the Soviet Union[70] and their attitude to democracy. My opinion is in all respects the opposite. Both positions are consistent. You, on the other hand, agree with Shouyi only in respect of your attitude to the world war; your attitude to the Soviet Union and democracy is apparently still close to mine, which I find truly incomprehensible. Please copy this letter to Zhao [Ji] and to Shouyi and the others. I hope that you will return to me the original, together with my earlier letters, for I plan at some future date to publish them. I enclose [Chen Qi]chang's letter. Greetings and good health,

Zhong

(September 1940)

---

70. I.e., that although it was degenerate and bureaucratised, it was still fundamentally a workers' state, in the sense that the legacy of the October Revolution had not been completely squandered and that the state that had resulted from it could still either go forward to real socialism by means of a political revolution or backward to the restoration of capitalism; and that it must therefore be defended against the bourgeois states.

My Basic Views[71]

This article summarises in thesis form the positions that Chen developed in his letters and articles before and after leaving prison: that the revolution is nowhere imminent; that war will merely simplify the structure of imperialism, not destroy it; that the bourgeoisie still has some progressive role to play; that Bolshevism has paved the way for Stalinism; that democracy is a universal mode of politics; and that the dictatorship of the proletariat is equal to the dictatorship of the Communist Party. Proletarian dictatorship is the very opposite of proletarian democracy, and thus of socialism, which is the economic complement of full democracy. Capitalism, in contrast, is the economic complement of limited, i.e., bourgeois, democracy. Chen adds that colonial peoples cannot hope to win national liberation in the absence of social revolutions in the metropolitan countries.

❧

(1) Revolutionary situations do not arise at any time and any place. It is preposterous to talk of a period of reaction as if it were one of revolution; i.e., to pretend that the ruling class is on the road to collapse when it is on the road to stabilisation after winning victory; to pretend that the middle classes are beginning to vacillate in their support for the ruling class when in reality they are vacillating in their support for the revolution, and starting to abandon its ranks; and to pretend that the revolutionary mood is rising when it has sunk into depression in the wake of a defeat. We must forget this nonsense about "the poorer people are, the more revolutionary they become". True, the law of physics that "every force has a reaction that is equal and opposite to it" can also be applied to society, but only on condition that the oppressed are sufficiently resilient.

(2) The proletarian masses are not at all times disposed to revolution, especially not in the wake of crushing defeats or at times of social or economic catastrophe.

(3) Without the numerical strength to match its social importance and without economic and political organisation, the proletariat is not so very different from other strata of the people. In particular the experience over the

---

71. Source: Zhuanji wenxue zazhi she, eds, *Shi'an zizhuan*, pp. 82–88.

last dozen or so years of bureaucratic rule in Soviet Russia and the experience of the Sino-Japanese War and of the present imperialist world war should caution us against overestimating the present strength of the proletariat in the world and lightly predicting the "imminent end of capitalism". Unless some world-shaking force intervenes, this world war will under no circumstances mark the end of capitalism and imperialism but will mark instead the second stage of its development, namely, from a plurality of imperialist states to the beginnings of a simple opposition between two imperialist blocs.

(4) We should strictly distinguish between the arbitrary "concentration" and "unity" of the petty bourgeoisie and the voluntary "concentration" and "unity" of the proletariat.

(5) We should strictly distinguish between the empty radicalism of the petit bourgeoisie and the straightforward determination of the proletariat.

(6) Now is definitely not the day of the final struggle, either in the backward countries or in the advanced countries of Europe and America. Those who arbitrarily proclaim that the bourgeoisie and the petit bourgeoisie are no longer in the slightest way progressive and have already absconded lock, stock, and barrel to the camp of reaction will simply capitulate in confusion when it becomes apparent that the bourgeois classes are still capable of playing a progressive role.

(7) We must grasp without prejudice the lessons of the last two decades and more of Soviet Russia. We must reevaluate in a spirit of scientific detachment, free from all religious passion, the Bolsheviks' theories and their qualities as leaders. It is quite wrong to blame every crime on Stalin, for example in relation to the question of democracy under the proletarian state.

(8) Democracy is the banner under which in every age, ever since humans first developed political organisation, right down until the withering away of politics (in Greece, in Rome, today, tomorrow), the majority class opposes the privileges of the minority. "Proletarian democracy" is no empty phrase. Its specific content, like that of bourgeois democracy, demands for every citizen the freedom to assemble, form associations, speak, publish, and strike; and above all the freedom to form a party of opposition. Without such freedoms, neither parliament nor soviet is worth a fig.

(9) Democracy (from a political point of view) and socialism (from an economic point of view) are complements and not opposites. Democracy is not indissolubly bound to capitalism and the bourgeoisie. If, in opposing the bourgeoisie and capitalism, the political party of the proletariat opposes

democracy as well, then even if so-called "proletarian revolution" were to break out in a number of countries, without democracy to act as an antitoxin to bureaucracy, they will be nothing more than Stalin-style bureaucratic states, brutal, corrupt, hypocritical, fraudulent, rotten, degenerate, and incapable of engendering any form of socialism. There is no such thing as "proletarian dictatorship" but only dictatorship of the party, which ends up as dictatorship of the leaders. All dictatorships are inseparable from brutality, fraudulence, corruption, and bureaucratic politics.

(10) Yes, the present world war is a war for world hegemony between two imperialist blocs. Yes, the so-called "war for democracy and freedom" is a facade. That does not mean, however, that there is not still a certain measure of democracy and freedom in Britain and America. In those two countries opposition parties, trade unions, and strikes are a reality and not a mere promise. Only a lackey of the Nazi fifth column would argue otherwise. It is even more unthinkable that America would use against the Isolationists[72] methods like those used by the Nazis against the Jews. Hitler's Nazis are out to rule the world with the same barbaric and reactionary methods with which they now rule Germany. In other words, they aim by means of a new and even more terrible Inquisition to impose everywhere one doctrine, one party, and one leader. They will not permit the slightest dissent, not even the existence of indigenous Nazi or Fascist movements in the countries they conquer. A Hitlerite victory will mean the stifling of all humankind, it will transform humans everywhere from thinking people endowed with free consciousness into unthinking mechanical beasts of burden void of free consciousness; so ever since the start of this world war and in future, too, progressive people of good intent in every country (including, of course, Germany) should make the destruction of Hitler's Nazis the general goal of a common offensive of all peoples; all other battles can only be deemed progressive insofar as they serve that general end. For once Hitler's Nazis win, all talk of socialism, democracy, and national liberation will be meaningless.

(11) In the present imperialist world war, to adopt a defeatist line in the democratic countries, a policy of turning the imperialist war into a revolutionary civil war, may sound left-wing but in reality it can only speed the Nazis' victory. For example, if the British government were toppled in a revolution by its own people, the British army, navy, and airforce would inevitably split

---

72. The Isolationists were Americans opposed to the US playing a central role in world politics; they believed that US resources could be better spent on solving domestic problems.

and become enfeebled, and the new revolutionary government would be in no position to nurture strong forces quickly enough to prevent a Nazi invasion of England. (Some people might object that "the defeat of one's own imperialist government is a lesser evil", in which case the Czechs and the French are indeed fortunate to be under Nazi occupation!) If you neglect the time factor, what might under other circumstances be true becomes preposterous. People rightly observe that the Sino-Japanese War has changed in nature as a result of the imperialist world war, but even so it would be wrong because of that to propose a defeatist policy in China and to work for the destruction of [Chiang Kai-shek's] Chongqing government. Under the conditions of today, such a policy would only hasten the victory of the Axis[73] – any other view is an illusion. For the same reason, we don't propose adopting a defeatist position in the Soviet Union, even though we have no reason to think that in the matter of human freedom Stalin's followers are any better than Hitler's.

(12) There is no reason to believe that preparing the revolution, i.e., uniting the masses, would be even more difficult in a state endowed with a certain measure of democracy than under the centralised rule of the Nazis; or that a Nazi victory would be more useful to the German revolutionary movement than a Nazi defeat. No one can foresee how long Nazi hegemony will last in Europe. To predict the inevitable collapse of Nazism in the wake of its victory and to use such a prediction as a justification for helping Hitler win whatever the cost in human sacrifice is a strategy of farce. It is on the same level as Stalin's policy at the time of the German coup of "letting Hitler take power", "he will soon lose power". In today's Europe, as in China during the Warring States period [475-221 BC] and Europe at the start of the modern era, economic development requires unity, and since there is no revolutionary unity, objective conditions may allow the Nazis to realise their reactionary unity. But such reactionary unity will not be able to shake off capitalism's economic constraints on productivity (the system of private property) in the way that feudal constraints on productivity (serfdom and the guild system) were shaken off during Europe's monarchical period; it will lack this progressive function. From a political point of view, the destruction of democracy and the restoration (for however short a time) of medieval reaction will be a terrible disaster for humankind and an incalculable loss.

73. In September 1940, Germany, Italy, and Japan signed the Tripartite Pact, which brought the Axis into being; the signatories promised to go to war against any nation attacking one of their number, save those already at war when the pact was signed.

(13) Only in countries inclined toward progress are war and revolution the product of the development of production and can become in their turn a cause of its further development; in declining countries, war and revolution weaken production even further, cause the national character and morals to become even more degenerate, grotesque, corrupt, wasteful, and unjust, and turn the political system into a reactionary military dictatorship.

(14) Only when two nations are equal in respect of weaponry and military techniques do the number of the armed forces, the degree of popular support, and the morale of the combatants count decisively toward who wins and who loses an international war. Even in civil wars the invention in the nineteenth century of new weapons obliged Engels to take a second look at the value of barricade fighting;[74] the invention of new weapons and techniques in the twentieth century will reduce even further the possibility of mass risings and barricades, unless splits occur in the ruling camp.

(15) Colonies or semi-colonies are a *sine qua non* of imperialism, as private ownership of property is of capitalism. It would be illusory to think that the system of private ownership of property will collapse without the collapse of capitalism, just as it would be illusory to expect the war for national independence in the colonies to win victory without first linking up with social revolution in the imperialist countries (the metropolitan states and their enemies). Today, with the Anglo-American and the German imperialists locked in a struggle to enslave the entire planet, an isolated national [liberation] war, no matter which class leads it, will either collapse altogether or will simply work a change (possibly for the worse) of master; even were the oppressed people to acquire a more enlightened master, one prepared to help stimulate political and economic development, it would work no fundamental change in its original slave status as a colony or semi-colony.

November 28, 1940

---

74. In his preface to the new German edition, published in 1895, of Karl Marx, *The Class Struggles in France*, Engels noted that after 1848, "rebellion in the old style, the street fight with barricades, which up to 1848 gave everywhere the final decision, was to a considerable extent obsolete".

LETTER TO Y[75]

In this letter, Chen seems to wish to reassure He Zhiyu that his letter to Hu Qiuyuan and Sun Jiyi (the next text in this volume) did not represent a break with Marxism.

❦

Dear Y,

I enclose my letter to H and S,[76] please forward it when you next correspond with them.... H and his ilk hope that I will quit the Marxist fold (so does Tao Menghe[77]), there's nothing strange about that, it's what they've always wished for. Our best policy is to discuss real issues (both historical and contemporary) with them so that they have no refuge. In order to avoid possible confusion, it's best not to enter the sphere of abstract theories and isms. Tao Menghe understood it rather well, while [Deng] Zhongchun[78] simply misunderstood.... I hope you are in good health.

Duxiu

January 19 [1941]

75. Source: Shui Ru, ed. *Chen Duxiu shuxin ji*, p. 513. This letter is not included in the Free China Press edition or in the Taiwan edition published by Zhuanji wenxue chubanshe. Y is He Zhiyu.
76. See the next letter.
77. Tao Menghe (T'ao Meng-ho) was a non-Marxist professor of sociology at Beijing University and a contributor to Chen Duxiu's *Xin qingnian* ("New Youth").
78. Deng Zhongchun, a medical doctor, was one of Chen's non-political admirers; Deng helped Chen greatly after Chen had moved to Jiangjin.

LETTER TO H AND S[79]

*In this letter, Chen informs his non-Trotskyist friends of his new view of Lenin
and Trotsky, and appears to abandon Marxist theory for a pragmatic approach
to political questions. See too his letter (not included in this volume) of December
23, 1941, to Zheng Xuejia, a former Trotskyist sympathiser who had later
become associated with the Guomindang, in which he rejects Marxism as irrelevant
not only to China but even to Russia and Western Europe. On the whole,
however, his final views are not irreconcilable with Marxism as Karl Kautsky and
others understood it.[80]*

❦

Dear Messrs H and S,

Three years have passed since I and Mr H parted, and it is more than twenty
years since I last saw Mr S. When I think back on my Beijing days [spent with
Mr S], I cannot but feel nostalgic.

I have seen your letters to Y and your comments on my latest works, I thank
you warmly for them. In formulating my opinions, I prefer to base myself on
the historical and contemporary process of events rather than on vacuous isms,
and I am even more loath to quote as a foundation for my thinking what
others may have said in the past. This method of "measuring by saints'
words"[81] is a weapon drawn from the armoury of religion, not of science.

In "My Basic Views", which I completed recently, I have also avoided
bringing in any sort of ism. My seventh thesis [in that essay] proposes reevalu-

79. Source: Zhuanji wenxue zazhi she, eds, *Shi'an zizhuan*, pp. 89-90. H and S are Hu Qiuyuan
and Sun Jiyi. Hu Qiuyuan was among the Chinese students who returned to China sometime
in the early to mid-1930s, after studying in Japan. The majority of these returned students
supported the Chinese Communist Party, but a few (notably Hu and Zheng Xuejia) showed
some sympathy for Trotskyism and borrowed weapons from the Trotskyist armoury to attack
the Chinese Stalinists. The leaders of the Communist Party were extremely hostile to Hu, Zheng,
and the other members of their group, and attacked them in an effort to discredit Chen Duxiu
and the real Trotskyists. Hu and his friends very quickly became associated with the Guomindang.
Hu earned his living by writing for the Shenzhou Publishing Company.

80. For Chen's letter to Zheng Xuejia, see Ren Jianshu and Tang Baolin, *Chen Duxiu zhuan*,
vol. 2,, p. 286.

81. A Buddhist term, meaning to take saints' words as the sole judgment and measure of truth
or falsehood, right or wrong.

ating the Bolsheviks' theories and leaders (including both Lenin and Trotsky) not by some Marxist measure but on the basis of the lessons of more than two decades of Soviet history. If the Soviet Union had rational grounds for existence (no matter whether it succeeds or fails), no one could repudiate it, even if its existence were not in conformity with Marxism. To confine oneself to a definite "circle" is to be "sectarian". The so-called "orthodox" is the equivalent of what the Confucianists of the Song dynasty called *daotong*.[82] None of these things were ever to my liking. That's why I came out against Confucianism when I found it to be wrong, and against the Third International when I found its policies to be wrong. And I'll take the same stance toward the Fourth, Fifth, and ...th Internationals. Shizhi[83] has called me "an oppositionist for life", and it's true, though not by my design; facts forced me along this road. Figuratively speaking, if meat tastes good, no one cares about which butcher sold it. But if it tastes bad and one still likes it simply because it was sold by Lugaojian,[84] that would be an exercise of superstition. Superstition and prejudice cannot withstand the test of events or the passage of time; I'll have nothing to do with either of them. That's all for now. Even from this [short letter], I trust you can discern my attitude in searching for the truth.

If I write new articles, I'll certainly send them to you for comments. I've a lot more to say, but unfortunately my poor health prevents me from writing. Moreover, even if I do write, it's very hard to get things mimeographed. Best wishes,

Duxiu (January 19 [1941])

82. I.e., the legitimate legacy of Confucianism.
83. I.e., Hu Shi (Hu Shih) (1891-1962), a philosopher, writer, advocate of the vernacular literature, and one of modern China's most influential liberal scholars. Hu taught at Beijing University from 1917 to 1927; between 1918 and 1920, he helped edit Chen Duxiu's *Xin qingnian*. After May Fourth, 1919, Hu split from Chen Duxiu and was strongly criticised by the Communists. He was a supporter of the Guomindang, and pro-American.
84. Suzhou's best-known cooked-pork shop, established several hundred years ago.

A Sketch of the Post-War World[85]

Here, Chen is at his most pessimistic. He doubts if the democratic countries can win the war, and predicts new world wars soon after the end of the present one; there will be no lasting peace, no justice, and no equality, either within nations or between them, whichever side emerges victorious. Imperialism will not weaken but grow stronger and bipolar: the post-war world will be divided between the hostile powers of America and Germany or of America and Britain; the two victors will attack one another and act as magnets for the lesser powers. Unless the "leading" countries go socialist (which Chen thinks unlikely, though he clearly hopes that it will happen), there will be no new independent states, for the Soviet example has shown that imperialism will not fall merely because its weakest link has snapped. Perhaps imperialism's resilience is in some ways a good thing, for economic unification is progressive even when achieved by counterrevolutionary force, and will inevitably pave the way to socialism. The Chinese people should resist imperialism, but they should at the same time learn from the West. They should seek to expand their industry in order to create the conditions for chiming in with future revolutions in the industrial countries. If the interests of nation and world democracy collide, the latter must take precedence.

❦

History does not repeat itself, and this present war has already caused huge changes throughout the world, or laid the basis for such changes. It is pointless to try to depict the future with theories drawn from the past.

There are only three possible outcomes to this war: neither Britain and America nor Germany and Japan will prevail, but both sides will talk peace; Britain and America will win; Germany and Japan will win. Least likely is the first outcome, so there is no need to speculate on it here. Of the second and

85. Source: Zhuanji wenxue zazhi she, eds, *Shi'an zizhuan*, pp. 91-103. During his last years in Sichuan, Chen generally made his views known not in public but through letters. This "Sketch of the Post-War World" is an exception. It was published in *Dagong bao* on March 21, 1942, just two months before Chen's death. The Guomindang refused to allow it to be published in Chengdu, apparently for fear of offending the Soviet Union, which Chen denounces in the article, and suppressed its sequel ("Once Again on the World Situation", the next text in this present volume). (See Ren Jianshu and Tang Baolin, *Chen Duxiu zhuan*, vol. 2, p. 298.)

third outcomes, which is the more likely? To judge by present conditions, it seems clear that Germany and Japan have the upper hand. The war has already been going on for more than two years. Having now acquired the support of the Soviet Union, for the last six months Britain has enjoyed a lull in the war, yet even with its entire forces it cannot block the advance of the numerically smaller German army in North Africa. It is hard to see how in the near future Britain can defeat the main German army. If one accepts that Britain's defeats in the various battle theatres have been due to the outnumbering of its army and its airforce, then within a year or eighteen months, after the British and Americans have had a chance to expand their arms production, there may well be a change in the overall situation. But today, although some people are calling for a "wholesale reorientation of factory production", to judge by the past and present behaviour of government officials – which was characterised by inertia – and factory owners, who care only about their own interests, it is doubtful whether Britain and America can succeed in beating Germany and the neighbours under its control in the arms race. And even if we do assume that at some future date they will be in a position to do so, are we also to assume that for some mysterious reason Hitler and his partners will simply bide their time and refrain from launching offensives in that year to eighteen months while Britain and America increase their armaments? Yes, Germany's internal crisis surpasses that of Britain and America, but it will only reach explosive proportions once war-weariness sets in or the German army is defeated. Germany's only weakness is its lack of oil. That is why Germany cannot sustain a long war unless it succeeds in capturing the Caucasus or Iran. For that reason, Germany needs a quick victory. The interest of Britain and America, on the other hand, lies in a protracted war. The main aim of both sides is to fix the time for action in their favour. So in Germany's imminent spring offensive, whether it happens in the Mediterranean or in European Russia, whoever is victorious along the line between Malta, Gibraltar, the Suez Canal, and Singapore or that between Moscow, the Caucasus, Iran, Iraq, Syria, and Singapore will have won the key to overall victory in the war. If the Axis powers win, Britain and America will be incapable of sustaining a protracted war. Throughout the history of warfare, space, numbers, and resources have never been the main factor in deciding victory.

If Britain and America win and the Axis powers are finished, new oppositions will arise at the peace table or the international conference to deal with the war's aftermath. It will not be easy for post-war Britain to clear up the

situation in Europe, North Africa, the Near East, and the Middle East, and
for a while its strength will not stretch to the Far East. The Far East, including
Southeast Asia and Australasia, is likely to become an American sphere of
influence. Under such circumstances, the friendship of Soviet Russia will be
a prize for which Britain and America compete; their fate will hang on the
next world war.

If Hitler wins the war, Britain will be finished, and America too will for the
time being be forced to withdraw to safety behind the Atlantic and the Pacific.
Even if Hitler does win, his guns will continue to point West, for he lacks the
military might to extend directly into the region to the east of the Urals, Iran,
and India. If such a time comes, then regardless of whether America and Japan
hold peace talks, America and Germany will vie for the friendship of Japan.
America will not necessarily continue to fight Japan, so until Hitler subjugates
America, he too is unlikely to risk offending Japan on account of the Far
Eastern question and driving his valued ally into the hands of the Americans,
thereby severing the right prong of his two-pronged offensive against America
from the Atlantic and the Pacific. Hitler knows that if, with Britain's strength
in the Far East destroyed, he were to threaten Japan, there would be the
danger of Japan and America cooperating, on condition that America with-
draws from the Far East. In that case, America and Germany's fate would hang
on the next world war.

It is still impossible to say how many more world wars there will be: all we
can say is that as long as the cause of war is not eliminated, wars will inevitably
happen, and that if Germany wins, the next war will come more quickly.
Evidently there will be no formal peace talks between America and Germany,
yet the actual fighting is bound to come to a temporary halt. And even though
Germany needs a respite from war so that it can set up its New Order, pluck
the fruits of victory, and (even more importantly) build sufficient numbers of
warships and cargo ships capable of crossing the Atlantic, once it had done so,
it would then restart the war against America, probably from South America.
Actually, every world war is nothing but a continuation of the previous world
war. We should under no circumstances allow ourselves to be befuddled by
high-sounding propaganda about "perpetual peace", "national self-determination", "the equality of nations", and "the destruction of the capitalist system";
under no circumstances should we believe that after the war these ideals are
likely to be realised.

The European and American project to reform capitalism is nothing new; however, it has resulted in the imposing emergence of the trusts alongside joint-stock companies and cooperatives; with labour legislation extended to half the world, in the so-called "socialist state" people have to restore the system of piece work. If reforming the system is not easy, destroying capitalism is even harder, and certainly not as effortless as some people imagine. When this war is over, not only Britain and America but also the Axis powers will inevitably try to reform the capitalist system, to make it more amenable to their rule. No one should be taken in by Hitler's denunciations of capitalism, they are simply his private joke. The reform project of all these states is simply to reduce barriers within each bloc by means of tariff agreements and even of economic unions, to diminish the role of currency by means of barter, and to nationalise some private firms. While tariff barriers within each bloc go down, those between the blocs will become intensified; not everything is barterable, and those goods that can be bartered are still valued in terms of currency, so it is still a sort of commodity transaction, not a form of division of labour. Even in the nineteenth century some industries were nationalised; wholesale nationalisation, i.e., so-called state capitalism, seems to be conceivable in theory but not in practice. If the cliques that control the means of production are not expropriated by revolution, there is no chance of them voluntarily handing over their private property to the state. Some people imagine that a "supra-class" government will peacefully expropriate private property, but any such government would itself be expropriated in double-quick time. So the three above-mentioned projects for reform are incapable of shaking the fundament of the capitalist system. Ever since capitalism first arose, its weals and woes have intensified in accordance with the logic of its internal development. Since reforms are incapable of disturbing its foundations, any measures to control it can only hasten the decline of the entire society and economy; to imagine that you can draw on its weals and avoid its woes is wishful thinking, it will get you nowhere. Private property and the commodity system are the basis of capitalism, and the root source of all capitalism's evils. The aim of the capitalist system of production is to augment the private wealth of those who own the productive means by selling its products as commodities, not in any direct way to satisfy the needs of the whole people. The more the productive forces develop, the more the laws of supply and demand – productive power and purchasing power – get out of kilter. The result is a crisis of overproduction, falling prices, factory closures, unemployment, and economic panic. After a while, the productive forces are restored to strength, and because they might now be even stronger than before, they lurch toward an even deeper crisis; hence the periodic law of cyclical crises. Usually there are two ways of coping with overproduction. One is the self-imposed reduction of the volume of production and even the destruction of products, a foolish and ridiculous method; the other is to conquer colonies, win markets overseas, and go to war, an insane and terrifying method. Because of the need to peddle surplus commodities on foreign markets and to stop foreigners invading the domestic market, tariff barriers are inevitably raised, armaments are increased, preparations are made for war, and in some cases hostilities begin. This chain of cause and effect inevitably binds present-day state authorities. For since they are incapable of destroying the capitalist system and instead allow it to lead them by the nose (any other response on their part would be defeated), this sequence of events is unavoidable – it cannot be changed by any ideology or moral principle. In an age when a number of strong states across the globe must vie for markets, prepare for war, and go to war, when they do everything in their power to extend their spheres of influence, when they are packed so tightly against one another that not a drop of water could trickle down between them, what point is there in talking about national self-determination or national liberation? At the end of the last war, [Woodrow] Wilson's Fourteen Points shook the entire planet; the reason they disappeared from the scene was not because [David] Lloyd George and Georges Clemenceau hoodwinked Wilson but because Wilson hoodwinked himself;[86] moreover, the deception led France to ruin,[87] and England and America were prevented from taking a strong stand toward Japan. After the present war, those who flaunt pacifist illusions in the capitalist world will be vanquished in the next war.

Will imperialist rule remain unchanged after the present war, no matter who ends up victor? As long as capitalism exists, imperialism, which is capitalism's natural product, will surely not reject itself. However, the actual form of

86. Wilson's Fourteen Points embodied the principles that he regarded as essential for a just and lasting peace after World War One and his wish for a world government that would prevent future wars. The Fourteen Points included the right to self-determination, which coincided with the aspirations of China's nationalist movement at the time. At the Paris Peace Conference in 1919, Wilson bargained away the Fourteen Points in deals with Lloyd George and Clemenceau, his wartime allies, who favoured a policy of peace-for-revenge, and disappointed the Chinese, thus triggering the events in China of May 4, 1919. People in China at the time felt that Wilson was a naive and idealistic scholar, ignorant of real politics, who deceived even himself.
87. I.e., France was defeated and occupied by Germany.

imperialist rule will inevitably change. Take, for example, the change from nation states to international blocs. Such changes by no means signal the end of the imperialist system; on the contrary, they show that imperialism is spreading and growing stronger. From now on, the pre-nineteenth century movement toward nation states will decline in the wake of the spread of imperialism, and the early twentieth-century opposition between seven or eight imperialist powers will also end. The Axis powers have belatedly completed the transition from nation state to imperialist state, Japan most recently of all. The imperialists are vying to grab the markets of the colonial and backward countries before anyone else gets hold of them. That is the sole reason they are prepared to take such risks, even to the point of trying to change the old imperialist world order by military means. This war will leave only two leading nations capable of complete independence and free from all alien controls, and those two nations – America and Germany or Britain and America – will be locked in opposition to one another. The peoples of all other countries will be subordinate to one or other of the resulting blocs, either as allies or as full-scale collaborators. Naturally Japan and Soviet Russia also aspire to lead their own blocs, but their fate will depend in the last resort on the level of their productive forces. As for the other colonial and backward countries, the age in which they might have hoped through the national struggle to form new independent states is already over. Within the blocs, countries can be roughly grouped into four categories, according to their strengths and weaknesses. The first category consists of relatively prestigious "allies", as Japan is for example to Germany and Soviet Russia is to Britain and America. The second consists of semi-colonies, for example Italy (in relation to Germany) and Holland, Belgium, and France (in relation to Britain and America); although these countries have their own governments, politically and (even more so) economically they are all more or less under the control of the leading nations. The third consists of dependent countries[88] like France and Belgium (in relation to Germany), Denmark and Italy (in relation to Britain),[89] and the Philippines (in relation to America); although they have their own governments, they are incapable of independent diplomacy. The fourth consists of the colonies, which lack even their own government and are controlled by governors from the metropolitan countries. There are none

88. I translate *beibaohuguo* as "dependent countries"; literally, it suggests "protectorates", a term that in this context carries the wrong connotations.
89. This passage is confusing: Italy belonged to the Axis and was not invaded by the Allies until July 1943; Denmark was occupied by the Nazis, like France and Belgium.

worse off than the colonies, unless it be the indigenous peoples of the Americas or of Australia. Though not all the nations and peoples in the two main blocs are alike in status, they have one thing in common, namely their political and economic systems are to a greater or lesser degree remade on the model of the leading nations. Systems that are absolutely contrary in character [to those of the leading nations] are inconceivable: in the German bloc, they are all modelled more or less closely on the Nazi system; in the Anglo-American bloc, on the democratic system. And the socialist system? Such a system can only be realised after the victory of the revolution in the leading countries, only then can socialism influence all the countries of the bloc. The experience of the Russian Revolution suggests that breaking the weakest link in the chain of world imperialism cannot eventually lead to the disintegration of imperialism as a whole. As for Soviet Russia today, it is not entitled to be a leading country, not only because of its low productivity but also because it has long since abandoned socialism.

At the start of this world war, some dreamers imagined that the chance had come for small, weak nations to achieve their independence. In reality, however, the colonies of Asia traded Anglo-American for Japanese control; and the colonies of Africa traded British for German and Italian control. Some people even imagined that the war would speed socialist revolution, but, to their great sorrow, things turned out differently; when they now discover that even the national struggle is labouring under constraints and that the Nazis are probably about to take over nearly half the world, they will plunge from their imaginary paradise into the deepest abysses, they will begin to believe that history is destined to go downhill. In reality, the history of human progress continues along its usual disinterested track, bound neither for paradise nor for the abysses of destruction; it bears not the slightest responsibility for the disappointment and sorrow that results from the destruction of the illusory hopes and joys of these people. Even if, by some tragic course of events, victory in this war were to go to the Nazis and half the world's population came under their domination, though politically this would result in a long period of catastrophic suffocation, it would have the same economic consequences as an Anglo-American victory. The Nazis would naturally be in no position to shake off the restraints imposed on productivity by the capitalist system, but a great step forward would be made within the capitalist system. For example, due to the unification of various currencies, the lowering of customs barriers, the concentration of resources, and so on, the number of the world's smaller economic units would be gradually reduced, thus removing some of the obstacles that have hitherto prevented economic development, and society's productivity would be increased much more rapidly than before the war. Objectively, this process would increase the material basis for broadening the road toward a socialist world, and is nothing more than capitalism's usual practice of creating progress by means of its bloody crimes: only a narrow-minded dogmatist would fail to see that. Human history is in this sense no different from the planet earth: it continues relentlessly on its path, whether at noontime or at midnight.

To be serious, genuine national liberation can only be realised in conjunction with socialist revolution in the imperialist countries. In a capitalist-imperialist world, "national self-determination" and "national liberation" for the backward countries and the weak nations is an illusion. The national struggle is even more likely to be restricted in an age like the present, when two rival imperialist camps compete through wars to force the backward countries and weak nations all over the world into war. Only a dreamer would be startled by such a comment. Looked at from the point of view of the progressive unification of the world economy, such constraints on the national struggle are not necessarily wholly bad. In the absence of revolutionary unity, even counterrevolutionary unity has a progressive significance, whether on a world scale or within a single country. For example, Wu Peifu's unity was better than the separatist warlord regimes, and Liu Xiang's was better than the age of "protection areas".[90] Moreover, to say that the national struggle will probably be to a certain extent restricted does not mean that nations led hitherto by other people will become as a flock of sheep, incapable of initiative. It simply means that the national struggle will meet with certain restrictions, the recognition of which is a precondition for effective action of the following sorts. (1) To work hard for the democratisation of the political system and the development of national industry, in order to increase the nation's weight within the bloc to which it belongs. Today is no longer the age of Li Hongzhang.[91] One should stop dreaming the pleasant dream that

90. Liu Xiang (1890-1938) was the most powerful of the Sichuan warlords in the 1920s and 1930s; while he (sporadically) held supreme power in the province, numerous smaller warlords each occupied and controlled a certain territory and designated it a "protection area".
91. Li Hongzhang (Li Hung-chang) (1823-1901) was a member of the faction that argued that China would have to achieve parity in industry and technology with the West if it was to remain independent and united under the monarchy. He and other members of his faction ran nearly all China's modern state-owned industries between 1860 and 1895.

[China] could become a rich, strong country at a single leap – that it could become an independent nation state like those achieved in the eighteenth or nineteenth centuries and become a first-class power in the twentieth century. (2) To create the forces (industry and national organisation) necessary for coordinating with the revolutionary struggle in the leading nations in order to achieve true national liberation and progress. It is wrong to dream of slamming the door shut, of eliminating imperialist might from a single country by the efforts of a single people in order to achieve independence for a national bourgeois state. (3) As for the struggle overseas, it should start out from the point of view of the interests not of nationalism but of democracy, regardless of whether this struggle is conducted against Axis or non-Axis powers, for the despotisms of Germany, Italy, and Japan, rampaging across the world hand in hand, have already broken through the last defences of the nations of the various countries. We are no longer talking about the fate of this or that nation but of the survival of freedom and democracy throughout the world. If we continue to fight our battles on national grounds, India's present enemy is Britain, and China will at some future point be forced once again to wage resistance, this time against America. (4) We must do all in our power to resist imperialist aggression, which threatens our survival as a nation, but we should not reject foreign culture. The conservative tendency to reject foreign culture can have only one effect: to cause one's own national culture, now stagnating, to decline. True, Chinese culture has its strong points, but taken too far,[92] it would look down on other branches of culture and even exclude from the notion of culture those technical-material achievements upon which the people's livelihood and national defence depend. As a result, there are people who even go so far as to exclude from the notion of culture glorious Chinese inventions such as printing and gunpowder, and instead reduce culture to art and literature. The baleful effect of this misunderstanding of the meaning of culture in the present Sino-Japanese War has been twofold. On the one hand, it has gratuitously transformed rhymers and scribblers into "people of culture". This is scarcely different from Japan's ironical remark that China is a country of words. On the other hand, by trying to resist warplanes, artillery, and tanks with the chanting of slogans and the singing of songs, it continues to promote the old Boxer idea that magic incantations can stop bullets; this is the impasse to which the lop-sided development of Chinese culture ultimately leads. Zhang Zhidong's harmful idea about "using Chinese learning for essentials

---

92. I.e., by exaggerating and one-sidedly promoting the humanities.

and Western learning for application" has already held us back for half a century.[93] By shouting about "our own culture" and "Oriental culture", we will similarly harm future generations of our people.

Some may consider that this war is a war between the imperialists of the Axis and the anti-Axis, with each side out to extend its own power and influence; it is not a struggle for national liberation; there is no point in small and weak peoples participating in it. This view is due to a failure to understand that although small and weak peoples cannot achieve their liberation by relying on imperialist assistance, they cannot resolve problems by their own efforts either. Moreover, at the present stage in the history of war, "neutrality" has become a thing of the past. If the people of Burma say, "Better the devil we know than the angel we don't know," we must reply: "We know of no angels in today's world, all we know is that the devil you know is ten times worse than the devil you don't!"[94] If some people in China say, "To help America defeat Japan is like chasing a tiger away from the front door and letting a wolf in at the back," we must reply: "If America wins the war, then we stand a chance of restoring our old semi-colonial status if we work hard to renew ourselves and stop conniving at corruption. But if the Axis wins the war, we will surely become a colony from which before long even the puppet government in Nanjing will be expunged!"

Some people may think that what I have written is too low-key: future events will teach them otherwise.

February 10, 1942.

93. Zhang Zhidong (Chang Chih-tung) (1837-1909) was a leading official who favoured reform, but warned against changes that would threaten Confucian culture, a position summed up in the slogan "Chinese values, Western means".
94. By "the devil you know", Chen means Japan. Some anti-colonialist Burmese leaders of the Dobama Asiayone or Thakin Party fell for Japan's "Asia for the Asiatics" propaganda and assisted the Japanese at the time of their overrunning of Burma in 1942. They were soon alienated by the behaviour of the Japanese occupiers.

ONCE AGAIN ON THE WORLD SITUATION[95]

In this article, Chen insists that the probability of a victory by Germany and Japan must not prevent the Chinese people from working for a British-American victory, if only to inspire the next generation of youth. To ensure collective security after the war, democrats must work toward a world federation, not an Asian federation that would exclude the rich countries.

❦

Some people say that the international situation as I described it in "A Sketch of the Post-War World", namely the possible prospect of a world wholly under imperialist rule, is too pessimistic. It seems to me that in assessing objective circumstances, important is whether or not you are realistic, not whether or not you are pessimistic. Ever since the late nineteenth century, finance capital has broken through national barriers and the world has been an imperialist world. That's exactly what imperialism is about. This is not something that relates to the future: the only thing that will happen in the future is that today's seven or eight imperialist powers will fight each other and consequently be reduced to two imperialist blocs. In the absence of a great revolution to shake the entire world, this state of affairs will continue and may even become worse than we have estimated. For should victory in the war go to Hitler, Britain will be finished, [Franklin D.] Roosevelt will fall to a Hitler of the Americas, and the next world war (between Germany and America) will be between two Fascist blocs rather than between democracy and Nazism. Then what Roosevelt said will have been proved right: that democracy and freedom will die out for several hundred years. In that case, the course of human progress could be plotted as follows.

Pre-Historic Antiquity
Clan democracy.

The Ancient World (Greece and Rome)
Democracy of the townspeople.

95. Source: Zhuanji wenxue zazhi, eds, *Shi'an zizhuan*, pp. 104–112.

.....

Autocracy of the great landlords, grand priests, and military leaders.

The Modern World
Bourgeois democracy.

.....

The feudal lords and (in the last phase) absolute monarchy.

The Future World
From proletarian democracy onward to democracy of the whole people.

.....

Fascist dictatorship.

According to this chart, Fascism, like other previous systems of dictatorship, would develop universally and come to constitute an entire historical stage, and democratic systems throughout history have always passed and will pass through a period of dark dictatorship. If people are content to sit back in their easy chairs and dream their optimistic dreams and thereby to let Nazism grow, we must be prepared to admit the possibility of such an age of darkness.

Although there should not be too great a discrepancy between objective evaluations and subjective efforts, they need not always head in the same direction. For example, even though we may believe that Germany and Japan are more likely to win the present war, that should not stop us in advance of the outcome from proposing that we do everything in our power to help Britain and America win; at the same time, our duty to work hard for the victory of our democratic allies should not lead us to believe that the Axis powers face inevitable defeat. We may pursue ideals, but we should not pursue completely unrealistic illusions; we should strive to advance ideals that are not absolutely unattainable, even though attaining them may still take many years, but we should beware of consoling ourselves with pipedreams. It is by no means a bad idea, when others set up comforting mirages and even abandon all vigilance, to paint the bleakest possible picture of events in the real world, in order to remind oneself of, and rouse others to, the need for even greater efforts. Rather than close one's eyes to the possibility of a world where imperialism reigns supreme, it is far better to stare hard at the tragic course of events and to admit that the danger exists that Fascist imperialist dictatorship might be universally established for an entire historic period. So in this present war we should do everything within our subjective might to rout Hitler and his accomplices and to penalise them with the utmost severity; we should inundate Fascist ideology with a great tide of democracy and freedom, so that after the war it is incapable of reviving under new guises in the victorious countries and of diverting the modern history of human progress along another path, in other words, so that we are not forced to live through an entire period of Fascist dictatorship and instead can pass directly into a world of extensive democracy; even if that is beyond the realm of the possible, we must still do everything we can, in the spirit of the old saying, "To do it even though we know it is impossible,"[96] to influence the next generation of young people to continue to fight to end Fascist reaction within the shortest period possible. That is the only ideal that we can possibly now pursue. To imagine that the present war can be transformed from an imperialist war into a war to over-throw imperialism everywhere is in all respects illusory. That is why I have braved the ridicule of old friends and backed the anti-Nazi alliance with Britain and America. Worst of all is to substitute an optimistic assessment of the objective world for subjective hard work; if before the present war [Prime Minister Neville] Chamberlain, Voroshilov, and Knox[97] had not chosen to view the enemy through rose-coloured spectacles, as not warranting an attack, and had instead made full military preparations rather than simply talking big, the war today would be going far better. For today's enemy is not like the stupid high officials of the Chancery of the Qing dynasty, who simply capitulated before the foreigners' braggadocio, nor can he be deceived by the passing [in parliament or Congress] of an empty bill for increased armaments or by the revelation of figures showing a rapid increase in arms production. The age of winning victories through sheer intimidation and deception is now past!

Litvinov's speech at a dinner party in the New York Club of Economists on March 16 [1942] was right on several points: "In my opinion the time factor is an unreliable and treacherous ally for both warring sides. We are on the one hand engaged in a prolonged war and on the other hand we are preparing military provisions and reserve forces to an extent surpassing that

96. A Confucian saying.
97. Marshall Kliment Yefremovich Voroshilov was Defence Commissar of the Soviet Union before and at the outbreak of World War Two. Colonel Frank Knox became US Secretary of the Navy on June 19, 1940. Actually, before his appointment Knox was known in the US as an internationalist, an opponent of the Neutrality Act, and a champion of compulsory universal military conscription.

of the enemy. Yes, we are on the right track in so doing; but such a plan can only serve its purpose if during the same period the enemy does nothing. You gentlemen know, however, that our enemies are not like that. They will build on their existing achievements to continue their advance, to continue to occupy territories, to gobble up new sources of raw materials, to enslave hundreds of millions of people, and even to acquire new allies. These advantages will inevitably far outstrip the advantages that our side acquires in terms of military preparations during this one-sided ceasefire." "If we console each other with empty talk about the impossibility of defeat, we will be even further from victory; this prospect causes us great anxiety."[98] This is a salutary if painful antidote to the frivolous optimism of those Americans and their allies who believe that "final victory will inevitably be ours" and "the Axis powers can only end in defeat". Let bygones be bygones, but we cannot afford to let the opportunity slip time and time again. If we wish to achieve final victory, we must strictly guard against empty optimism. Compare, for instance, the speech delivered at the same New York Club of Economists by [Viscount] Halifax (identified by British public opinion after the Battle of Dunkirk as one of the appeasers in the cabinet of Chamberlain) with that of Litvinov.[99] [In the light of such attitudes], we must even more surely root out [excessively] optimistic opinion, treat it as an enemy, and make doubly sure that we substitute for it the following theses.

(1) Britain and America should not be suspicious of Russia, but should provide large-scale aid to the Russian army so that it can hold on to Moscow. They should not (to quote Litvinov) "deploy their best-equipped forces in places where there is no fighting". Nor should they believe the nonsense about Russia having already demonstrated in the course of the war that its forces outstrip those of Britain and America, that it is in a position to rout Hitler. Least of all should they delude themselves into thinking that the successful defence of Moscow is in only Russia's interests. Higher arms production is vital for an Allied victory, and time is needed to produce arms. Halifax said optimistically: "Militarily and industrially, America still has latent potential." He forgets that we cannot magically transform that latent power overnight into weapons. Hitler has postponed his spring offensive until the summer. His target is probably still Moscow. Only if Moscow can be defended for a year

98. This speech by Litvinov has been retranslated into English from Chinese.
99. Maksim Maksimovich Litvinov (1876-1951) was Soviet Ambassador to the USA from November 1941 to August 1943.

or eighteen months, so that Hitler is unable to switch his forces to the south, will America and Britain have enough time to increase the level of their arms production above that of their enemies. Otherwise, the fall of Moscow and the routing of Russia's crack troops in accordance with Hitler's plans will enable Hitler to take advantage of his victory to move his troops south toward the Caucasus, Iran, and Iraq and to join forces with Japan at Suez in order to blockade the Mediterranean. If by then Britain and America have still not increased their arms production, the game will be as good as lost!

(2) Arms production cannot be raised by empty words. There are not at present enough arms factories to match and outstrip the enemy in this regard, nor is there enough time to build new ones. The only solution is "compulsory reassignment", i.e., switching other factories as far as possible to producing armaments. There can be no final victory until our arms production outstrips that of the enemy. At this point I fear that some people will object that I am a proponent of the theory that "weapons alone decide the outcome of war". Actually, ever since the invention of flint arrowheads, victory or defeat in war has depended increasingly on arms, to the point where today it is virtually true to say that war is a competition of arms. The heroic yet tragic defeat of France at Sedan and of Britain at Dunkirk and in Malaya and Singapore proves the truth of this axiom. Opponents of the theory that "weapons alone decide the outcome of war"[100] are no less vociferous than others in demanding tanks and planes of the Americans; they too prove my point.

(3) The experience of the League of Nations shows that both to win victory in a war and to ensure collective security after it one must organise an international bloc capable of leadership and endowed with an economy and armed forces that are strong enough [to carry out its decisions]. The passage from the growth of nationalism to that of a new international collective is not only inevitable but is a prerequisite of human progress, a prerequisite – we must do all in our power to replace Fascism with a democratic bloc – of the transition to a world federation. [Jawaharlal] Nehru's proposal for an Asian bloc[101] without Britain and America sounds nice, but its only real effect would be to prolong Asia's backwardness; and like the Burmese theory of "sooner

---

100. Evidently a reference to the Chinese Communists, in their wartime capital of Yan'an.
101. Nehru's strong pan-Asian feeling found expression at around this time in his call for an Eastern Federation, in which India and China would be the senior partners. Nehru had earlier argued that India should play a crucial role in the Afro-Asian world. Nehru's attitude toward the war (when he was imprisoned by the British) was that if India were to participate enthusiastically in the anti-Fascist struggle, it would first have to be granted freedom.

the devil you know", it's a racialist prejudice that can only help boost Japan's "Greater East Asian Co-Prosperity Sphere".[102] We must dispel such noxious illusions! For to imagine, in a world bent on war, that there might happen a rising of armed masses independent of the two imperialist blocs is either an illusion or conscious fraud. Nehru's proposal for Asian independence does not share the same motive as Subhas [Chandra] Bose's[103] call for Indian independence, but its effect will be the same: to give succour to Germany and Japan.

(4) Since we are participating in the anti-Nazi struggle led by the democratic arsenal of America and in an Allied bloc battling to protect democracy and freedom throughout the world, naturally we must make democracy and freedom the central thought of our compatriots so that all concentrate on the same militant goal: China's economic backwardness, its [undemocratic] tradition, and the war situation we are now in must not prevent us from creating an ideal system of democracy and freedom. That fact is obvious, but we must at the very least express the determination to carry on down the road toward democracy and freedom. We should not be like those people who oppose democracy and freedom root and branch, who denounce democracy and freedom as clichés, and who say that those of us who favour democracy and freedom are living anachronists; or who, a little less bluntly, oppose Chinese-style "democracy and freedom" to the basic principle of democracy that underlies the world's democratic countries; they share in common the belief that democracy is no longer appropriate to the modern state, by which they indisputably mean Germany, Italy, and Japan (with or without Russia), definitely not Britain and America. By adopting such an attitude [toward democracy and freedom], will the progressive Chinese in general fail to understand to what end we make our War of Resistance against Japan a part of the war against Germany, Italy, and Japan? Will they succeed in dissipating China's determination to see this war through to the end? Will they manage to assist our enemies' sinister and contemptuous denunciation of America for "aiding non-democratic nations with democratic goods and materials"? And,

102. The "Greater East Asian Co-Prosperity Sphere", an extension of Japan's anti-Communist "New Order in East Asia" proclaimed in November 1938, envisaged in 1940-1941 including China, the mandated Pacific islands, all of Southeast Asia, and even Australia and New Zealand in a self-sufficient economic system free from Western exploitation and under Japanese political hegemony.
103. Subhas Chandra Bose (1897-1945) was a leader of the Indian Congress Party who broke with the majority of the Congress leaders and tried to achieve India's independence with the help of Japanese imperialism. He led an Indian national force against the West during World War Two.

finally, will they succeed in causing our allies to distrust the sincerity of our adherence to the democratic alliance? These are questions that we should deeply ponder. Perhaps some people believe that the only conceivable future is a Fascist world, and not just for a limited period of time; that democracy and freedom will be dead forever. This is simply speculation, without any basis in facts or history. It is simply an ideology; it cannot be designated either as pessimistic or as optimistic.

April 19, 1942.

Zheng Chaolin, circa 1930

Chen Duxiu (left) and Peng Shuzi in 1932, at their trial in Jiangning

Leon Trotsky, Mexico, 1939 (photo courtesy of Alex Buchman)

The Provisional Central Committee of the (Trotskyist) Communist League of China, winter 1936. Clockwise from left: Wang Fanxi, Frank Glass, Hua Zhenlin (not a CC member), Han Jun, Chen Qichang, Jiang Zhendong (photo courtesy of Alex Buchman)

Chen Duxiu, circa 1937

Chen Duxiu. Chen's own penned caption reads: "Taken in the First Nanjing Prison in the spring of the 26th year of the Republic" (i.e., 1937)

Zheng Chaolin, circa 1985

Wang Fanxi, Leeds, England, 1989

THE FUTURE OF THE OPPRESSED NATIONS[104]

In this article, Chen retreats somewhat from the reservations he seemed to express in "Once Again on the World Situation" about the usefulness of uniting oppressed nations. Though he continues to insist that some imperialists are worse than others, he also says that all movements of oppressed peoples against imperialism must be supported and oppressed workers and peoples everywhere must unite to that end, in order to bring about world socialism. But only a revolution encompassing "advanced" as well as "backward" countries can lead to the development of the economies of the poor countries; in the absence of world revolution, imperialism will help forge the links that create such unity. National liberation will follow from world socialist revolution, just as the abolition of unequal treaties in China followed on the October Revolution in the years before it degenerated. Struggles for national liberation can no longer proceed in separation and isolation from one another: people everywhere will have to become free together, in an international socialist federation. This argument is the late Chen's clearest and most trenchant restatement of his commitment to Marxist internationalism and the Trotskyist theory of permanent revolution, and of his undying hostility to capitalism and imperialism.

᪅

The oppressed nations are the product of capitalist imperialism. The oppressed toilers produce commodities for imperialism; the oppressed peoples of the backward nations buy commodities from the imperialists and produce raw materials for them. These are capitalist imperialism's two props.

It is only natural that oppressed peoples should resist oppression by capitalist imperialism even to the point of going to war against it. There can be no blame in such conduct. Every progressive member of the nation should support such struggles for national freedom, regardless of who leads them. For even a national liberation struggle led by the bourgeoisie, even one led by the feudal nobility, is progressive insofar as it strikes a blow at capitalist imperialism.

But what will be the future of such a struggle if it stays confined within the bounds of a national struggle?

(1) From a national angle, experience suggests that war is not only incapable

104. Source: Zhuanji wenxue zazhi she, eds, *Shi'an zizhuan*, pp. 113-120.

of making a nation less backward but will even make it more so. Quite apart from setting back political and academic thought, a protracted war will lead to a blockading of the economy and to inflation. In the absence of social sanctions, and given the weakness of our political organisation, it is easy for corrupt officials, unscrupulous merchants, and landowners to use the sheer chance created by national hardships to collect windfalls by engaging in the hoarding and cornering of goods; and owing to their crimes, our resistance fighters are dying in pools of blood at the front and our common toiling people starving and suffering in the rear. Should you propose applying more or less unpeaceful methods to change this state of affairs, people will scream at you that you are exceeding the bounds of national struggle and sabotaging the national front against the invader. And in fact these methods do exceed the bounds of national struggle. Yet to let things go on as at present is precisely to deal a fatal blow to the war of national liberation. At the same time, these awful things cannot be done away with by resorting to propaganda and persuasion or to decrees issued by the government. What is to be done?

(2) From an international point of view, today, when the imperialists are competing for colonies and the market in the backward countries is greatly intensified, according to Gandhi one nation cannot gain freedom by depending on aid from an [imperialist] power; and he is one hundred per cent right. Yet nor can it without the assistance of one of the powers free itself from the present oppression of another power. What's more, some powers will come to your assistance whether or not you depend on them to do so; that too is an incontrovertible fact. At this point Nehru has no way out. Perhaps there is a slight difference between him and Gandhi, in the sense that he is not suggesting that American aid be rejected. Should America enter India, we know that its stance on the colonies is better than that not only of the Axis powers but even of Britain; the Philippines are a case in point, although they cannot be considered an independent nation-state. For the Indians to exchange British for Japanese rule on the grounds of national independence would be an even greater disaster. However much Gandhi and Nehru stress in their propaganda that the age when Indians will acquiesce in foreign oppression has now passed, they must know in their heart of hearts that they cannot simultaneously expel the British and repulse Japan and Germany. The outcome would simply be to languish under the rule of a new master and to [have to] continue with the campaign of civil disobedience. Well, what is to be done?

In my opinion, therefore, in the present world of capitalist imperialism, no small or weak nation is in a position to close itself off or to rely on its own national resources to expel all imperialist invaders in order to realise an independence of this sort. The only real way forward is to unite with the oppressed toilers and the oppressed and backward peoples of the entire world to overthrow imperialism everywhere, and in so doing to replace the old world of international capitalist commodity exchange with a new world of international socialism based on a division of labour and mutual aid. When that happens, the national question will solve itself.

There are two conceivable objections to such an opinion. Some may ask how a backward nation can speak of socialism, and how it can unite with the toilers of other nations and with small or weak nations; others, whether socialism implies national liberation.

Those who raise the first objection are blinkered by the old nationalist viewpoint. They are unable to see the future trend toward ever-greater internationalisation. It is, of course, self-evident that the backward countries themselves, given their economic state, are in no position to speak of socialism, or even of capitalist development. Today the backward countries, whether out to develop capitalism or socialism, can do so only in reliance on the advanced countries. Only an obsessive nationalist would believe otherwise. Over the last hundred years, capitalism's colonial policy has already breached the Great Wall that surrounded backward nations everywhere. After this war, the form of imperialist rule will in all cases change from a policy of colonialism to one of an even more concentrated and organic international bloc. Talks about the so-called Atlantic Charter, Pacific Charter,[105] and the like mark the start of that process toward a reconstitution into blocs. If, after the defeat of the Nazis, Germany were to emerge as a socialist state leading an international bloc, some advanced countries would before long fuse with the backward countries in a socialist federation. Even in an international bloc led by capitalist imperialist countries into which backward countries are absorbed and where they are forced to cooperate in every respect with the leading countries, even under that sort of unequal cooperation, the working people of the backward countries and the leading countries would get the chance to unite with one

---

105. The Atlantic Charter was drawn up by Franklin D. Roosevelt and Winston Churchill in August 1941 as a joint statement of principles for which to fight the war and on which to base the peace; it was a first step toward founding the United Nations. The Pacific Charter was either a projected Pacific version of the same thing, thought up in Chongqing or Washington, or Chen's rhetorical invention.

another, leading to a huge concentration of the oppressed, a force brought into being by the imperialist robbers that will lead eventually to their own downfall. No nationalist hero will be capable of holding up this new trend toward the formation of international blocs. As for the oppressed peoples, only if they know how best to accommodate to this new trend will they have a future.

Those who raise the second sort of objection have been befuddled by the theories of the Second International.[106] The project of the Second International is to pursue a reform campaign within the confines of bourgeois rule; being one of the props of imperialism, it has paid no attention to the question of the liberation of the oppressed nations. A true socialist movement wishes to overthrow international capitalist imperialism root and branch. That is why, ever since the First International, "the liberation of the oppressed toiling peoples" and "the liberation of the oppressed nations" have been the two banners of this movement.[107] Once socialist revolution succeeds, as long as it does not change colour in mid path it will be unable to coexist for long with the system of commodity and money. When such a time arrives, will there still be oppressed peoples? This is not just a theory, but was the actual experience of Russia's October Revolution. The October Revolution was the achievement of the overwhelming majority of the Russian people united under the three great banners of the Communist Party: "liberate the toilers", "liberate the peasants", and "liberate small nations". After the victory of the revolution, each of these three slogans was realised: they were not just dud cheques issued by the Russian Communists. What's more, the voluntary abolition was proclaimed of all unequal treaties forced on other countries during the Tsarist period. One by one the Communists announced the relinquishment in oppressed countries of Tsarist privileges such as settlements and consular jurisdiction.[108] As a result, working people and oppressed nations

---

106. The Second International (1889-1914), though never a uniform, centralised organisation like the Third, was dominated by the figure of Karl Kautsky, who transformed Social Democracy into a movement of reform on which revolutionary slogans were mere ornaments. At first the Second International opposed militarism and espoused internationalism, but when war came in 1914, most socialist parties obeyed the call of the fatherland; the Second International collapsed, and Lenin decided that the time had come to found the Third.

107. "The problem of the liberation of the oppressed nations" was raised by Lenin and the Third International. Marx' slogan was "Workers of all countries, unite!" Lenin's was "Workers of all countries and oppressed nations of the world, unite!"

108. I.e., of extraterritoriality. On July 25, 1919, the Soviet Government in Russia declared the abolition of the unequal treaties signed between Tsarist Russia and China and the privileges enjoyed by Russia in China (though in practice it hung on for a while to some of them).

throughout the world came to see Moscow as a beacon for the oppressed peoples of the world, and as the general headquarters of the world revolutionary movement. If some people, on the basis of recent Soviet policies toward the Sino-Japanese War and, at the start of the conflict, toward Poland and Hitler, are sceptical about the attitude of socialist countries to the liberation struggle of oppressed peoples, that's because they are confused! There is a world of difference between the Soviet Union of the early days, which we support and others defame, and that of the latter period, which they flatter and we deplore. The Soviet Union of the early period stood on the side of world revolution; of the latter period, on that of Russian national interest. Since then, the Soviet leaders, in view of the setback of the revolution in Western Europe, have turned their coats when midway toward their goal and switched their main focus from world revolution to defending Russia's national interest; as a result, perceptive people everywhere have gradually become sceptical and finally disillusioned, so that by now, although people in their heart of hearts still cherish some measure of hope for the Soviet Union, in reality they have no choice but to admit that it is simply one among the world powers. Anyone who continues to insist that the Soviet Union is a socialist country can only do so by perverting the very meaning of socialism! Were Russia today still abiding by its old position of international socialism, then once war broke out between China and Japan, it would have supported China with all its might, i.e., not like Britain and America, who back China in a detached sort of way, but as if the responsibility for leading China's resistance against Japan were Russia's own, by committing troops to take part in the war, by living or dying together with the Chinese people. This would be the only truly internationalist standpoint; no other standpoint would befit a truly leading nation! Had that happened, Japan would have found it harder to occupy Shanghai and Nanjing. If Moscow had stopped appeasing Japan at the very start of the Sino-Japanese War or, at the very least, after the outbreak of clashes between the Red Army and the [Japanese-backed Chinese army] at Zhanggufeng,[109] Wuhan would not have fallen. And had China and Russia continued to resist shoulder to

---

109. In late July and early August 1938, Japanese troops provoked Soviet troops at Zhanggufeng on the border between China, Korea, and the Soviet Union. The Japanese were defeated, and sued for peace. On August 11, in Moscow, both sides agreed that a mixed commission of two Soviets and two representatives of Japan and the Japanese puppet regime of "Manchukuo" would investigate and settle the border question in the region. The Zhanggufeng Incident at first gave heart to some Chinese, who thought that a Soviet-Japanese War would break out and enable China to go onto the counter-offensive against Japan.

shoulder to this day, Japan would have been in no position to rampage through Southeast Asia and to devastate a whole number of small, weak nations such as the Philippines, Malaya, Java, and Burma! When the Nazis invaded Poland, if the Soviet Union had still stood on an international socialist position it would not have compromised with Hitler and would not have described the role of representative democracy and the great cause of leading all oppressed and invaded nations to fight against the Fascist offensive as pulling the chestnuts from the fire for someone else, and it would have been even less likely to gang up with the Fascists to divide Poland! At that time, the British, French, and Belgian allied army had not yet disintegrated, and Hitler had not yet convinced himself that he was capable of simultaneously winning victory on the Eastern and the Western fronts. Only after the defeat of isolated Poland and the absence of any further problems in the Eastern battle theatre did Hitler have the strength to rout the British, French, and Belgians and to vanquish a host of small nations such as Norway, Holland, Denmark, Yugoslavia, and Greece.

These historical stories alone, which show how the different positions taken by Russia in its earlier and later days brought different results, are quite enough for us to understand the relationship between international socialism and the oppressed nations.

Given that, in European terms, Russia is itself after all a relatively backward nation, what will be the outcome of its whole policy on the national problem? In order to protect itself, Russia substituted a policy of compromising with Fascism for one of attacking it; as a result, the war in Russia began not when Hitler was isolated in Europe but after Hitler had routed the European nations. Hitler has occupied not only half of Poland and the three Baltic countries, which had been offered to Russia as the price of Russian compromise with Fascism, but also most of European Russia. But for the help of Britain and America, even Moscow might by now have fallen. In the interests of its own security, Russia has all along avoided going to war against Japan, so that even the Chinese Communist Party has been accused of "roving around without fighting".[110] The result is, despite Russia's standby attitude, that Japan will still help Hitler attack Russia tomorrow, thus plunging the Russian people into a state of great insecurity. When that time comes, Russia will miss the support of China, having sat back and watched while Japan crippled China. So any

110. This is a pun, directed by the Guomindang against the Communists, on *youji*, "guerrilla warfare", literally "to rove and attack".

backward nation that confines its policy entirely to one of the pursuit of national interest will inevitably become isolated and bereft of any future, for a national policy is in reality a policy of isolation. This goes for Soviet Russia too.

May 13, 1942.[111]

111. Fourteen days before Chen's death.

LETTER TO Y[112]

A fortnight before his death, Chen arranges for his article on "The Future of the Oppressed Nations" to be sent to his non-political friends, but not to the Trotskyists in Shanghai, who (he says) will neither understand nor agree with it.

🍂

I've got the letter you posted when you returned to your school,[113] thanks. I hope that you will send me the copy of *Jiangjin ribao* ["Jiangjin Daily"] that XX[114] brought for you. I don't intend to send any articles for publication in that newspaper. XXX will soon be leaving. XX has already left for India, I mentioned this in my previous letter, I hope you've already received it. One might say that the article I sent you[115] is a recapitulation of the previous three essays,[116] or, rather, a word or two to clinch the arguments I advanced in them. Please show the two widows[117] this article. I leave it to you to decide whether or not to send a copy to XXX. If you do decide to do so, perhaps they can then send it on to XXX. It's unnecessary to copy it to anyone else,[118] since copying is not easy and, even if they get a copy, they will not understand and

112. Source: Zhuanji wenxue zazhi she, eds, *Shi'an zizhuan*, pp. 121-122. Y is He Zhiyu.
113. He Zhiyu, who was at the time teaching in a middle school in Jiangjin, had paid Chen a visit and then gone back to Jiangjin.
114. The people referred to in this letter as XX and XXX are impossible to identify, save that they were Chen's personal and non-political (or no longer political) friends. These people maintained contact with Chen but were afraid to make this contact public, lest they be discriminated against or persecuted, by either the Guomindang or the Communist Party. To hide their identity, the original editor erased their names when he included this letter in the collection.
115. "The Future of the Oppressed Nations" (note by the original editors).
116. "My Basic Views", "A Sketch of the Post-War World", and "Once Again on the World Situation" (note by the original editors).
117. A nickname, it is not known whose.
118. Obviously a reference to the Trotskyists, most of whom at the time were in Shanghai.

agree with it. I no longer have a copy of the third article ("Once Again on the World Situation"), please return the original to me. I've got the letter you posted when you arrived back at your school, thanks.

Good health,
Duxiu.
May 13, 1942.[119]

119. Chen Duxiu died on May 27, 1942. As he himself said, these articles and letters "are merely my personal opinion, they represent no one else" (see his letter to [Chen] Qichang) and others "will not understand and agree with it" (see his letter to Y). (Note by the original editors, January 28, 1948.)

APPENDICES

Appendix 1

CHEN DUXIU HAD NO WISH TO REJOIN THE CHINESE COMMUNIST PARTY ON LEAVING GAOL[1]

Zheng Chaolin

This article was completed on August 10, 1981, two years after Zheng Chaolin himself had emerged from twenty-seven years in prison under the Chinese Communists and while he was under Party supervision and denied access to the archives. On the basis of the scant documentation available to him he builds a strong case for "historical truth" and against received opinion regarding Chen Duxiu's view of the Communist Party in 1937.

❦

Just as many people claim that Chen Duxiu was dismissed as General Secretary [of the Communist Party] by the August 7 Conference [of 1927],[2] so for several decades now people have been saying with one voice that after his release from a Guomindang gaol in 1937, Chen expressed a wish to return to the Communist Party; but Mao Zedong raised three conditions and wanted Chen publicly to repent his errors, which Chen did not do, so Chen did not rejoin. Not only Communist Party members say this; so do some democrats, and they have even been joined by the ex-Trotskyist Pu Qingquan.[3] In his article "Chen Duxiu As I Knew Him",[4] Pu ascribed the following words, told in reported speech, to Chen: "I definitely want to return to Party work." In this way, Pu "proves" the groundless rumours of that period. But when he

1. I translated this article from its unpublished manuscript version, titled "Chen Duxiu chuyuhou jue wu fuhui Zhonggongde yuanwang" ("Chen Duxiu definitely did not wish to rejoin the CCP after leaving prison"); at some point, the article was published under the same title in *Zhongbao yuekan* (Hongkong).
2. According to Zheng Chaolin, Chen Duxiu resigned before the conference; see Zheng Chaolin, "Chen Duxiu and the Trotskyists," p. 135. See also C. Martin Wilbur, *The Nationalist Revolution in China, 1923-1928*, Cambridge: Cambridge University Press, 1983, p. 144.
3. I.e., Pu Dezhi.
4. See Pu Qingquan, "Wo suo zhidaode Chen Duxiu ("Chen Duxiu as I knew him"), *Wenshi ziliao xuanji* ("Selected materials on literature and history") (Beijing), no. 71 (1980). Pu's article was reprinted in four instalments in *Zhongbao yuekan* (Hongkong), also in 1980.

was a Trotskyist, Pu gave no credence to these rumours. I shall clarify this question by discussing a few facts.

I myself have never believed these rumours, and I always considered that they were not worth discussing. In recent years, however, more and more people have started doing research on Chen Duxiu, and nearly all of them believe the rumours to be true. The time has therefore come to clarify the matter and save from further error those who now and in the future engage in research on Chen and on this period in Chinese history.

No, between leaving gaol and dying, Chen never entertained the idea of rejoining the Communist Party. The idea never once occurred to him after he had embraced Trotsky's proposals and worked in the Trotskyist organisation.

Personally, I have not the slightest doubt of this. I do not need to consult a single document or fact; I base my conclusion solely on his usual conversations with us [before we went to prison]. On September 29, 1937,[5] the day I was released from prison, I went to stay at his residence and had a talk with him. Our talk proved to me that he had not changed; as a result, I am even more firmly convinced of my opinion on this matter.

But I cannot expect to convince others to share my firm belief simply by referring to conversations that Chen had with several of us before going to gaol and to a talk he had with me on the first night after my release. Elsewhere, I have already explained on the basis of our conversation that evening that after leaving prison in 1937 he had not the slightest intention of rejoining the Communist Party.[6] Here, today, I do not intend to base my argument on that talk, because it can convince only me. Instead I shall provide more objective evidence.

The best proof that Chen Duxiu expressed no wish to rejoin the Communist Party after leaving gaol in 1937 can be found in Chen's own words. In Hankou in [March] 1938 he wrote an open letter to *Xinhua ribao* in which he said: "According to Luo Han, they still hope I will rejoin the Party."[7] In other words, he himself did not hope to "rejoin the Party", but the Communist Party hoped that he would, and moreover had dropped Luo Han a hint along these lines.

5. Writing in "Chen Duxiu and the Trotskyists," p. 183, Zheng Chaolin recalls that he was freed from gaol on August (not September) 29, 1937.
6. See Zheng Chaolin, "Chen Duxiu and the Trotskyists," pp. 183–184.
7. Chen Duxiu, "Gei *Xinhua ribao*de xin" ("Letter to *Xinhua ribao*"), reprinted in Zhang Yongtong and Liu Chuanxue, eds, *Houqide Chen Duxiu*, pp. 112–133.

Let us see what light Luo Han's famous "open letter"[8] throws on this question. In August [1937], after the start of the battle for Shanghai, Luo Han came to Nanjing. Chen Duxiu was still in gaol at the time, and Luo did not visit him. He went directly to the Eighth Route Army office at Fuhougang in search of Ye Jianying.[9] At the time of the Northern Expedition, Luo had been "Party representative" (or "director of the political department") of the Fourth Army of the [Guomindang's] National Revolutionary Armed Forces, at the same time that Ye Jianying (if my memory serves me rightly) was its chief of staff. The two men were naturally close to one another. Luo Han had two aims in going to the Eighth Route Army office: first, to ask the Communist Party to do what it could to get the Guomindang to release political prisoners, including Chen Duxiu and the other Trotskyists still in gaol; and, second, to repeat the old proposal of 1932, when the Trotskyist organisation had formally suggested bilateral cooperation with the Communist Party against Japan. In 1932, the Communist Party had ignored the proposal, but now that it was working together with the Guomindang against Japan, Luo Han, acting in his personal capacity, revived the proposal. This shows that Luo Han's proposal referred to the question of the Trotskyists and the Communist Party working together against Japan, and not to the question of Chen Duxiu or other Trotskyists "rejoining the Party". Luo Han spoke very clearly about this to Ye Jianying in Nanjing and to Lin Boqu[10] in Xi'an, and Ye and Lin heard very clearly what he had to say. Luo Han declared several times that he represented only himself and not the Trotskyist organisation or Chen Duxiu. Lin Boqu said: "Since you are only setting out your own views, in a personal capacity, and do not enter into discussions in a representative capacity, things could as well be settled by radio communication."

Even so, [the Communist leaders in] Yan'an did not completely believe what Luo Han said, and still thought that he was representing Chen Duxiu. They therefore set three conditions for Chen's "capitulation". That is to say, even though the two sides would be merely cooperating, Chen would still have to repent his errors and oppose Trotskyism. It is also possible that Yan'an actually thought that Chen Duxiu had sent Luo Han, to discuss not just cooperation but "rejoining the Party". All these things passed through a series

8. On April 24–25, 1938, Luo Han published an open letter to Zhou Enlai and others in *Zhengbao* ("Upright Daily"). See Feigon, *Chen Duxiu*, p. 223, fn. 73.
9. The Eighth Route Army was formed in 1937 on the basis of the old Red Army; Ye Jianying was the Communist Party's representative in Nanjing.
10. Lin Boqu (1896-1960) was a veteran Party leader.

of lips and finally reached the conclusion that Chen Duxiu would repent his
past errors and return to the Party ranks. (During a talk between Wang
Ruofei[11] and Luo Han, Wang said something about sections of the Third
International not admitting members of the Fourth International; this remark
was precisely a reference to this question of "rejoining the Party".) Chen
Duxiu did not repent, whereupon the rumour-mill again began to grind: Chen
Duxiu had been unable to accept the three conditions, so he had not been
allowed to rejoin the Party.

From what I have said above, we can see that all this talk about Chen Duxiu
wanting to rejoin the Party or go to Yan'an is Communist Party propaganda
without any basis in fact.

Some people might, of course, object that I base my argument solely on
letters of Chen Duxiu and Luo Han, that I have absolute faith in their veracity,
and that I completely ignore Communist Party documents that provide
evidence to the contrary.

Regarding such documents, I have access only to Ye Jianying, Bo Gu, and
Dong Biwu's letter to *Xinhua ribao*.[12] I don't even have the other articles
published in *Xinhua ribao* on this question. So I can quote only from Ye, Bo,
and Dong's letter.

This letter was written in reply to Chen Duxiu's open letter to *Xinhua ribao*.
It says: "At the beginning of September, after his release from gaol, Chen
entrusted Luo Han to talk with us, and told us that he wanted to return to
work under Party leadership." This statement can, of course, be interpreted
as meaning that "Chen wished to rejoin the Party". There is a difference
between this statement and what Luo Han said in his "open letter". Luo Han
declared that he was acting on his own account, whereas this letter says that
he was representing Chen Duxiu; Luo Han said that he had gone to negotiate
cooperation, this letter says that he transmitted Chen Duxiu's wish to return

11. Wang Ruofei (1896-1946) joined the Communist Party in 1922 and was a member of its
Central Committee until 1945. He died in a plane crash in 1946. While in Moscow in 1928
as a member of the Chinese delegation to the Comintern, he had secretly expressed sympathy
for the Trotskyist Opposition.
12. Bo Gu (1907-1946), the alias of Qin Bangxian, had been acting General Secretary of the
Chinese Communist Party from 1932 to 1935. Dong Biwu (1886-1975) was a veteran
Communist, and became a Central Committee member after 1945. The two men were members
at the start of the war of the Party's Changjiang Bureau, set up to represent the Party and lead
its work in central and southern China. The letter by Ye, Bo, and Dong referred to here is
reprinted in Zhang and Liu, eds, *Houqide Chen Duxiu*, pp. 235-236. See Feigon, *Chen Duxiu*,
p. 223, fn. 73.

to work under Party leadership. So who is right and who is wrong? I believe Luo Han to be right, since he gives dates. He went to Nanjing to talk to Ye Jianying in August [1937], before Chen Duxiu had left prison; he left Nanjing for Xi'an on August 30, arrived in Xi'an on September 2, met Lin Boqu on September 3, received Yan'an's three conditions on September 10, and returned to Nanjing on September 15, by which time Chen had already left for Wuhan. In the week from August 23, when Chen left gaol, and August 30, Luo Han did not meet Chen Duxiu. This is understandable, since he did not know where Chen lived. I was at Chen's house the whole of August 29, day and night; I did not meet Luo Han, nor did anyone else mention him.

Ye, Bo, and Dong's letter goes on to say:

> After Luo had left Nanjing, Chen also sent Mr Li XX [i.e., Li Huaying][13] to hold talks: Mr Chen had already broken decisively with the Trotskyists, and urgently wanted to meet us. We took the view that this would be difficult, since Chen had not publicly set out his political position. Mr Li XX said: what Mr Chen wants is precisely to explain his political position to us, so Bo Gu and Ye Jianying met Mr Chen. We requested him to explain his attitude to the anti-Japanese national united front and to leave the Trotskyists.... Afterwards, Chen again sent someone to say that because Li XX had been at the meeting, Chen had found it difficult to speak freely, so he asked to see [Ye] Jianying a second time. At the meeting, Jianying asked Mr Chen publicly to express to the entire nation his opinion on three points.... [Dong] Biwu too met Chen in Hankou to urge Mr Chen to fulfil these three conditions.

These three meetings all ended inconclusively. Even more noteworthy, in the course of them Chen Duxiu expressed no wish to "rejoin the Party". So apart from the opening sentence about Chen wanting to "return to work under Party leadership", what other support does this letter provide for the claim that Chen wanted to "rejoin the Party"? (As I have already explained, even this sentence is unreliable: Luo Han had not met Chen in Nanjing, so there was no way that he could have received a commission from him.)

What is more, the claim that Chen wanted to "return to work under Party leadership" is open to another explanation: the "united front" entailed various groups and parties working together with the Communist Party yet outside the Party, but it also entailed these groups and parties "working under the leadership of the Party". Ye, Bo, and Dong deliberately used this ambiguous formulation in their letter, and for the following reason: neither Chen Duxiu nor Luo Han had spoken of "rejoining the Party", so if Ye, Bo, and Dong had

13. The given name was added by Zheng Chaolin; it is not clear who Li Huaying was.

said "Chen wants to come back into the Party and work under the leadership of the Central Committee", their statement would have had no basis in fact.

If Zhang Guotao's memoirs are to be believed, Yan'an discussed Chen Duxiu's case in terms of "cooperation" and not of "rejoining the Party".[14] Recalling the Politburo Conference of December 1937 in Yan'an, Zhang notes a speech by Wang Ming:

> We can cooperate against Japan with anyone except the Trotskyists. Internationally, we can cooperate with bourgeois politicians, warlords, and even anti-Communist executioners, but we cannot cooperate with the followers of Trotsky. In China, we can cooperate with Chiang Kai-shek and his anti-Communist special agents, but we cannot cooperate with Chen Duxiu.

Finally, I would like to mention the attitude of the Trotskyist cadres, who were concentrated in Shanghai. At that time, Peng Shuzhi's supporters and his opponents were equally dissatisfied with Chen Duxiu's activities in Wuhan. But they only opposed Chen's wish to cooperate with the Chinese Communist Party and not his alleged wish to "rejoin the Party". They found it completely inconceivable that Chen would wish to "rejoin the Party". On November 21, 1937, Chen wrote to Luo Shifan, Chen Qichang, and Zhao Ji:

> About cooperating with the Stalinists, my view is that there's nothing wrong with it in principle, but at present it's out of the question. To cooperate, both sides must have something to give; in addition, there must be some common activity that necessitates both sides getting in touch – yet at present such conditions do not obtain. Naturally it's crazy to talk of "cooperation"; Luo [Han] didn't mention this matter to me, you have no cause to get oversensitive about it.[15]

In other words, Chen Duxiu was not opposed in principle to cooperating with the Communist Party against Japan, but saw such cooperation as conditional on our having a certain strength, and on the necessity of constant contacts with the Communist Party arising from the anti-Japanese activities. At the time, that condition was absent, so Chen opposed cooperating with the Communist Party. So he would have been even less likely to want to "rejoin the Party". If those "oversensitive" individuals had suspected that Chen was inclined to "rejoin the Party", rest assured that they would have raised a great hue and cry.

14. Zhang Guotao (1897-1979), a founder of the Chinese Communist Party and one of its principal leaders, left the Party in 1938 and retired from politics. His memoirs appeared in English as Chang Kuo-t'ao, *The Rise of the Chinese Communist Party*, 2 vols, Lawrence, Kansas: University Press of Kansas, 1971-1972. Wang Ming (1904-1974) was Stalin's chief supporter in the Party leadership.
15. See the "Letter to Chen Qichang and Others" in this volume.

Chen Duxiu's letter proves even more conclusively that Luo Han's actions in Nanjing and Xi'an were his own personal initiative. After he had met with a rebuff and gone to see Chen, he "never talked about" the cooperation.

Whether we are dealing with big matters or small, we should always stick to the historical truth. Anything that does not accord with historical truth should be pushed aside, even though people repeat it as if with one voice. Some may consider that it is a minor question, not worthy of detailed study, whether or not Chen Duxiu expressed a wish to "return to Party work" after his release from gaol. But in my opinion, from the point of view of the struggle of the Chinese Trotskyists, of Chen Duxiu's character, and of Chen's relationship with the Chinese Trotskyists, it is no minor matter, but one that requires thorough clarification on the basis of historical evidence.

Appendix 2

LETTER TO FRANK GLASS[16]

Leon Trotsky

Trotsky's letter to Frank Glass (Li Furen) in Shanghai is by way of a reply to Chen Duxiu's letter to Trotsky (the second document in this selection) of November 3, 1938, which Glass had forwarded on Chen's behalf on January 19, 1939. Trotsky had expressed worries about Chen's physical security as early as 1937, and had become even more worried after April 1938, when Wang Ming and Kang Sheng started up a campaign in China to slander Chen as a "paid agent of Japan". He was therefore keen to get Chen to America, where he would be both safe and able (so Trotsky hoped) to play the same role in the Fourth International as the Japanese Katayama Sen had played in the Third. In a letter accompanying Chen's, Glass, commenting on Trotsky's efforts to persuade Chen to seek sanctuary in the United States, had said that Chen "does not believe as Crux [Trotsky] did that he is in imminent personal danger from the Stalinists or the Kuomintang [Guomindang]" (since, as he says, the numbers and present influence of the Fourth Internationalists in China "are not such as to invite strong attack".[17] According to one source, Chen did not rule out a sojourn in the United States, and even tried to obtain a passport; he desisted only because his health deteriorated and, moreover, because it soon became clear to him that the Guomindang would under no circumstances let him leave China.[18] But Wang Fanxi, Chen's collaborator and correspondent in those years, believes this assertion to be untrue. Trotsky died in Mexico, at the hands of an assassin, on August 20, 1940.

🐦

16. The original of this letter, written in English, is held in the China files of the "Exile Papers of Leon Trotsky", deposited at Harvard University and made accessible in 1980.
17. The full text of Frank Glass' letter to Trotsky is translated into French in *Cahiers Léon Trotsky* (Grenoble), September 1983, no. 15, pp. 113-118.
18. Peter Kuhfus, "Chen Duxiu and Leon Trotsky: New Light on Their Relationship," *China Quarterly*, June 1985, no. 102, pp. 253-276, at pp. 273-274.

March 11, 1939.

Dear Friend,

It was with the greatest interest that I read your letter from Shanghai of January 19th and the statement [by Chen Duxiu] from Szechwan [Sichuan]. At last we have the information we lacked until now. I am very glad that our old friend remains a friend politically in spite of some *possible* divergences which I cannot appreciate now with the necessary precision.

Of course, it is very difficult for me to form a definite opinion on the politics of our comrades or the degree of their ultra-leftism, and thus on the correctness of the sharp condemnation on the part of our old friend. However, the essence of his statement seems to me to be correct, and I hope that on this basis a permanent collaboration will be possible.

I continue to believe that the best thing for him would be his sojourn in the [United] States for a period. Do you not believe that it would be feasible even without the approval of the high authorities?

I cannot share his optimistic view that no danger threatens him now. Yes, for a period our Chinese comrades are protected to a small degree by their own weakness. However, we are becoming stronger and stronger internationally. Our party[19] has begun to play a serious role in the States. It is a tremendous warning to the Stalinists and they will try to prevent a similar danger in the other countries. They will begin with the most prominent figures of our movement.

My warmest greetings and good wishes.

      Comradely,
        T[rotsky]
Coyoácan, D. F.
2-5

19. A reference to the Socialist Workers Party, at that time the American section of the Fourth International.

Appendix 3

MY FEELINGS ON THE DEATH OF MR CAI JIEMIN[20]

Chen Duxiu

"Who since ancient times has not died?"[21] Life is short, and death counts for little, yet I cannot help but grieve the death of Cai Jiemin, not only because of his contribution to the public weal, but also on account of the personal relationship between us! Thoughts and feelings about society and politics over the last forty years!

The first time I collaborated with Mr Cai was in the last years of the Guangxu reign [1875-1908] of the Qing dynasty. In those days, Yang Dusheng, He Haiqiao, Zhang Xingyan,[22] and others in Shanghai launched an organisation committed to studying the use of explosives in a projected campaign of assassination. Xingyan wrote a letter inviting me to join, and once I had reached Shanghai from Anhui, I did so. I stayed in Shanghai for more than a month, and each day I experimented together with Yang Dusheng and Zhong Xianchang[23] in manufacturing explosives. Mr Cai too used to attend frequently in order to conduct experiments and get together for a chat. The second time I collaborated with Mr Cai was from 1916 to 1918, at Beijing

20. Source: Zhuanji wenxue zazhi she, eds, *Shi'an zizhuan*, pp. 123-127. This obituary was added by Hu Shi or his friends in Taiwan to the Free China Press edition of Chen Duxiu's last writings; it is absent from the original Shanghai edition. Cai Jiemin is another name of Cai Yuanpei (Ts'ai Yüan-p'ei) (1868-1940), who was a member of the Shanghai group of terrorist assassins (which Chen Duxiu briefly joined) and a supporter of Russian nihilism before he joined the Guomindang, of which he became a veteran leader. Cai was China's most outstanding liberal educationalist. He sponsored the May Fourth (or New Culture Movement) around 1919 in his capacity (between 1916 and 1926) as Chancellor of Beijing University. He founded and became President of the Academia Sinica.
21. A line from a poem by Wen Tianxiang, a national hero and poet captured by the Mongol army and finally put to death because he refused to serve the new Yuan dynasty. The following line says, "Let my red heart glitter in history."
22. Zhang Xingyan (1872-1973) (another name of Zhang Shizhao) achieved fame as a journalist, writer, and politician. He was one of Chen Duxiu's old friends, but his politics were extremely unstable. He changed from a radical into a conservative, and from a cabinet minister in a warlord's government into an admirer and supporter of Mao Zedong.
23. A member of the Shanghai terrorist group.

University. That period of joint activity lasted relatively long, and I got to know him much better.

Generally speaking, Mr Cai was a benign and uncontentious person, a lovable man who would offend no one. Sometimes, however, when his moral integrity or some matter of principle was at stake or when he had already resolved on a certain course of action, he became stubborn and unbending and was no longer prepared to accommodate others, even though he continued to adopt a mild and gentle attitude. That was the first thing that caused people to admire the old gentleman. After the Reform Movement of 1898,[24] Mr Cai himself often inclined toward the new progressive movement, but while he was President of Beijing University, he employed all sorts of people whose scholarship he admired: not only [radicals like] Hu Shi, Qian Xuantong,[25] and Chen Duxiu, but conservatives like Chen Hanzhang and Huang Kan[26] and even people such as Gu Hongming[27] (who wanted to restore the Qing) and Liu Shipei[28] (who participated in the Hongxian movement[29]). Such magnanimous toleration of dissident and alien viewpoints and respect for academic freedom of thought is rare among Oriental people, who are accus-

24. The Reform Movement, inaugurated by Kang Youwei in 1895 and supported by Liang Qichao, Tan Sitong, and other leading thinkers of the time, advocated the transformation of Confucianism into a religious movement, to provide the basis for modernising the state and the education system and for establishing representative institutions. It came to an abrupt end in 1898, when the reactionary Empress Dowager, Cixi, carried out a coup against Kang and his supporters.

25. Qian Xuantong (Ch'ien Hsüan-t'ung) (1887-1939) became an anti-Manchu revolutionary in 1903 and later leaned to anarchism. He taught linguistics at Beijing University. During and after the May Fourth period, he played an important role in reforming written Chinese and in propagating the new culture in general. In some respects he went even further than Chen Duxiu and Hu Shi. Later on, however, he devoted himself entirely to the study of ancient Chinese history.

26. Huang Kan (Huang K'an) (1886-1935) was a leading disciple of Zhang Binglin (1868-1936), the famous classical scholar and revolutionary; in 1915 he recommended Qian Xuantong to Beijing University.

27. Gu Hongming (Ku Hung-ming) (1857-1928), born of Chinese ancestors in Penang, Malaya, was known as an "imitation Western man"; he was fluent in several European languages but not in Chinese. He wore a queue and hated both foreign colonialism and Chinese republicanism.

28. Liu Shipei (Liu Shih-p'ei) (1884-1919) was an early Chinese advocate (in Japan) of socialism. At first he was an anti-Manchu revolutionary. Later he became a conservative literary man and favoured the restoration of the monarchy in China.

29. In August 1915, Yuan Shikai, president of the newly established Chinese Republic, launched a movement to restore the monarchy, with himself as emperor. He announced as his reign title "Grand Constitutional Era" (*Hongxian*), which was to begin with 1916. Within six months, Yuan was discountenanced and dead; his Hongxian dynasty lasted a mere one hundred days.

tomed to despotism and respect only what is orthodox. That is the second thing that caused people to admire the old gentleman even more.

Now that Mr Cai is no longer with us, his friends, his students, and all those who recall him should bear in mind these two virtues!

After Mr Cai passed away, an old fellow-student of mine at Beijing University wrote asking me to compose an obituary for Cai, to be published in a special issue dedicated to Cai's death, and added: "Ever since May Fourth,[30] some people have recommended the casting aside of national essence and morality. Perhaps in your essay you can show how that is wrong and indicate the right path."

On this question, my opinion is as follows. All peoples worthy of the name have their culture, or their national essence; in the great furnace of world cultures, the culture of each people, insofar as it is of value, i.e., insofar as it can be called national "essence" rather than national "dregs", is not easy to melt down. Even if a people becomes extinct, its culture may live on. The question is whether a national culture is preserved in the hands of the nation itself. If a people becomes extinct, or even if it is not yet extinct, and its culture or national essence is preserved by the people of another nation, that is truly catastrophic. Only in this sense does "preserving the national essence" have meaning. If some people view national culture in isolation from world culture and national essence in isolation from world learning, and with closed eyes extol themselves and deprecate everything foreign, shutting the city gates to keep out foreign science, even to the point of refusing to use foreign scientific methods as a tool for sorting out Chinese knowledge, then all our learning will have lost the advantage of comparative study; it will be impossible to choose the best of it and expound it comprehensively. Those who embrace as national "essence" what are in effect national "dregs" and who advocate reading aloud from the Confucian classics while remaining wholly ignorant of the textual knowledge and real meaning contained in them are truly frightful!

---

30. In 1914, Japan seized German-controlled territory in Shandong. In 1917, Britain, France, and Italy secretly agreed to support Japan's claim to this territory, and in 1918 the Government in Beijing secretly acquiesced in this decision; in 1919, the Paris Peace Conference agreed to transfer German rights in China to Japan. On May 4, 1919, three thousand students demonstrated in Beijing against this "national betrayal", and in the course of the demonstration beat a pro-Japanese official. There followed a nationwide movement of strikes, lecture-strikes, and anti-Japanese boycotts. On June 28, the Beijing Government gave in to the protest movement and refused to sign the Peace Treaty with Germany. So the May Fourth Movement in its narrowest sense had been brought to a successful end. In its broadest sense, May Fourth was a movement of cultural renewal and revolution that lasted roughly from 1917 to 1921.

In human society, besides law, morality is an indispensable cement. Those who fundamentally deny morality, whatever class or party they belong to, are shamelessly wicked and base-minded. However, morals, unlike truth, were formed to meet social needs, and are bounded by time and space. What this person sees as moral, that person may not; what people in the past saw as moral, people today may not. For example, widow-burning was considered moral in old India, but not in China, where widows were expected to live chastely after the death of their husband. A widow who remarried was considered immoral in China but not in the West, and even in China today it is no longer considered as something extremely bad. To kill a person is the most immoral thing of all, but in battle he who kills or wounds the greatest number of people is a hero. Stories about burying the living along with the dead and cutting off pieces of one's own flesh[31] as an act of loyalty or filial piety used to be told with approval. The idea, imported to China from the West, of equal rights for men and women was naturally highly incompatible with China's ancient morality, i.e., the ethical code of Confucianism; even so, members of today's Chinese gentry no longer publicly defend to the death the old system of morality. As a matter of fact, to practise equal rights between men and women, the virtue of self-restraint is necessary on the part of the men. In short, morals change according to the age and the social system; they are not immutable and frozen. Morality is a form of self-discipline and not an obligation that you simply impose on others. It requires that you practise what you preach; it should not be empty verbiage designed for the purposes of self-glorification. The louder people shout about morality in a society, the more backward and degenerate that society will be. On the other hand, the personal conduct of the great scientists of the West is no worse than that of the sanctimonious priests and pastors, while that of the philologists[32] of the Qing dynasty was much better and more honest than the ethical intentions of moralists like Tang Bin[33] and Li Guangdi.[34] As for Mr Cai, he proposed replacing religion with aesthetic education. He opposed the worship of

---

31. A so-called "filial son" would cut small pieces of flesh from his arm or leg, mix them with medicinal herbs, boil the mixture, and serve it to his ailing parents as a drink.
32. *Puxue*, a scholastic tendency devoted to philological research, mainly into the Chinese classics, and spurning speculative philosophy supposedly based on those classics.
33. Tang Bin (T'ang Pin) (1627-1687) was an orthodox early-Qing Confucian.
34. Li Guangdi (Li Kuang-ti) (1642-1718) aspired to be known as a follower of the Song philosophers, though he was accused of paying more attention in practice to his career than to the Confucian dictate of filial piety.

Confucius and he never preached morality, but his moral quality far surpassed that of many of those who constantly go on about morality.

This is not just my personal opinion. I daresay that on these two questions my position is more or less identical with that of Mr Cai and Mr Hu Shizhi. Shizhi is still alive. If you don't believe that our views are more or less identical, you can go and ask him. And anyone intimately acquainted with Mr Cai's words and actions will know that what I have said about him is not mere rubbish.

The May Fourth Movement was an inevitable product of the contemporary development of Chinese society. Whether one views it as an achievement or as cause for blame, it should not simply be attributed to those few people. However, Mr Cai, Shizhi, and I were principally responsible in those days for articulating intellectual opinion, and since the public has raised doubts about important questions, in the absence of Shizhi (who is abroad),[35] I – as the sole survivor still resident in China – have no choice but to venture a few passing comments in this brief essay for the public of today and of tomorrow, and in commemoration of Mr Cai![36]

35. Hu Shi was Chinese Ambassador to the USA from 1938 to 1942.
36. The original text can be found in *Central Daily News*, Chongqing, March 24, 1940 (note by Hu Shi).

Appendix 4

ORATION AT THE FUNERAL
OF MR [CHEN] DUXIU[37]

Gao Yuhan[38]

Place: School in Jiangjin,[39] Deng's villa.
Time: Noon, June 1, Year 31 of the Republic [1942].

I would like to express on behalf of [my dead friend] Mr Duxiu and his family
and relatives sincere thanks to the venerable Mr Deng Chanqiu, a leader of
the Jiangjin gentry, and his respectable nephew Mr [Deng] Xiekang [for all
that they have done for Mr Duxiu]. At the same time, and in the same way,
let me thank Mr Sun Maochi, Chairman of the Board of Directors of Jiangjin's
Yucai Middle School, and other gentlemen. When news that Mr Chen had
fallen ill reached town, Mr Deng Xiekang, together with Mr Zhou Fuling and
me, went down to the village to pay Mr Chen a visit. After that, Mr Xiekang
discussed with me what to do with Mr Chen's remains; he resolutely assumed
responsibility, without waiting for anyone to ask him to do so. After returning
to Jiangjin, he rushed around attending to Mr Chen's affairs, leaving himself
little time to eat or sleep. He arranged the funeral vestments and the coffin
to everyone's perfect satisfaction. In the meantime, some difficulties that arose
concerning the procurement of the coffin were solved only after Mr Deng's
tireless pleading and persuasion. The venerable Chan[qiu] is already more than
seventy years old and living in retirement at Baisha Village, but as soon as he
heard the sad news of the death of Mr Chen, he hurried to Jiangjin, and, after
setting foot ashore, rushed without resting to Mr Chen's death bed at Heshan-
ping to express his condolences. Regarding the grave, Mr Xiekang had already

37. Wang Shudi et al., eds, *Chen Duxiu pinglun xuanbian* ("Selected appraisals of Chen Duxiu"),
2 vols, Henan: Henan renmin chubanshe, 1982, vol. 2, pp. 406–410. This memorial address
was originally published in *Dagong bao*, Chongqing, June 4, 1942.
38. Gao Yuhan (Kao Yü-han), an old friend of Chen's who had studied in Germany, was a writer
and author of *Baihua shuxin* ("Letters in the vernacular"), a veteran revolutionary, and a political
instructor at the Whampoa (Huangpu) Military Academy. He is famous as the first Communist
openly to attack Chiang Kai-shek, as "the Southern Duan Qirui". (Duan Qirui was a leader
of the Beiyang warlords in the north.) Gao became a Trotskyist in 1929.
39. Jiangjin is a town near Chongqing, Sichuan province; Chen Duxiu lived in the countryside
outside Jiangjin between 1938 and his death in 1942.

generously decided to turn his newly built villa – Kang Garden, situated at the side of Peach Tree Forest outside the Great West Gate – into Mr Chen's graveyard, and the venerable Chan has readily assented. At the same time, Mr Sun Maochi, Chairman of the Board of Directors of Yucai Middle School, representing the Middle School, generously offered to reserve a suitable plot of land in the school grounds in which to bury Mr Chen's coffin and remains; and to erect in the vicinity of the grave several buildings in which to display items left behind by the deceased, in order to give people an impression of what he was like while alive. These acts of friendship are born of simple and unaffected sensibility of a kind that cannot be won by force; in the modern age, such noble acts and feelings are as rare as the feather of a phoenix or the horn of a unicorn, and would have been rare too even in antiquity. Now that it has finally been settled that Mr Chen's grave will be in the grounds of Mr Xiekang's villa, things have happened as if predetermined: Mr Chen lived for four years in Jiangjin, during which time, the two Messrs Deng – uncle and nephew – of all the gentlemen in Jiangjin became his most intimate friends. Mr Chen several times went walking with the venerable Chan in the Peach Tree Forest; last spring, Mr and Mrs Chen, together with Mr [Zhou] Fuling and me, came to inspect the blossom and to gaze down at the great Yangtse River; we were captivated by both trees and water – so great was our delight that we lingered on, forgetting to return. Who could have guessed that the place where Mr Chen came to delight his eyes would also be the place where he closed them in eternal sleep? Were Mr Chen conscious in his grave, he would experience complete satisfaction. And the noble and generous example of uncle and nephew Deng will last forever!

But it is my belief, shared, I am sure, by all, that Mr Chen, by lying here, will at the very least not sully the worthy owner's pure soil, or fail to live up to the majesty of the mountains and rivers of this place. Mr Duxiu is at home everywhere, and naturally an adherent of the view that "my bones may be buried no matter where among the green mountains". Now that he sleeps peacefully here, it can truly be said that he rests in the right place. Considering the [grandiose] outlook he ever held, the [miserable] conditions he was recently forced to live in, and his perspective on the [present national and international] situation, we might console ourselves with the thought that he left the world at the proper time. In the moment before he passed away, I am sure that his conscience was completely clear. At this point, friends present will naturally turn their thoughts to the question of how to appraise Mr Chen's life. In regard to his learning, his cause [as a revolutionary], and his entire personality, and on the basis of his posthumous works and the inerasable imprint that he has left on the history of Chinese politics, culture, thought, and social movements over nearly forty years, people in the future will certainly make a fair appraisal of him. As for me, I want to raise three points that, as a crude sketch, will perhaps help Mr Duxiu's mourners here today understand what made him the man he was.

First, I wish to look at Mr Duxiu's position in the history of culture and thought. We must absolutely avoid [approaching any historical figure by distorting – not to say fabricating – his or her achievements, by either] exaggerating or belittling [them]. However, one thing is undeniable, namely, that during the May Fourth period it was he who solemnly raised the two slogans:

Support Mr De (Democracy);

Support Mr Sai (Science).

In those days, when Liang Qichao,[40] Zhang Junmai [Carsun Chang],[41] and others were zealously advocating metaphysics and the Beiyang warlord government[42] was fighting its last struggles, Mr Duxiu's sharp eyes had already seen what China's people and China's cultural and intellectual world urgently required; i.e., he had already fully realised that if China was to free itself from the two heavy weights of warlordism and colonialism and to build an independent and free nation, politically it required democracy, while culturally he urgently called for science so that the country could be industrialised. Ever since, everything that we have struggled for, including the war of resistance that the government is urging us to wage, take as their guiding principle these two slogans. So Mr Duxiu's position in the history of culture and of thought is not difficult to understand.

40. Liang Qichao (Liang Ch'i-ch'ao) (1873-1929), a journalist, historian, and constitutional monarchist, became leader of the so-called Study Clique after the downfall of the Qing dynasty. In 1919, during the May Fourth Movement, he questioned "the dream of the omnipotence of science". In 1923, he supported the conservative view that China should value its own spiritual civilisation.
41. Carsun Chang, a student of Henri Bergson and Rudolf Eucken and founder (in 1934) of the Chinese National Socialist Party (which became the Democratic Socialist Party in 1946), felt that after May Fourth, too many Chinese believed that science could solve all problems. He argued in 1923 that science, being applicable only to dead matter, "is not able to solve the problem of a view of life", and he questioned the value of a material civilisation achieved by science.
42. During the warlord era (1916-1928), Beijing was in the hands of a succession of rival militarist cliques.

Second, I wish to look at Mr Duxiu's position in China's new literary movement. Naturally, the new literary movement was part of the cultural movement, but since the present generation of Chinese young people has not yet completely understood the emergence and development of this movement and its enormous influence on new China, it is worth dwelling on it for a moment. Everyone knows that Messrs Chen Duxiu and Hu Shi were pioneer advocates of the new literary movement, but it is not generally known that Mr Duxiu championed the new literature[43] long before the May Fourth Movement, and even long before the 1911 Revolution.[44] While running the *Anhui baihua bao* ["Anhui vernacular magazine"] in Wuhu,[45] he already made clear his determination to reform Chinese literature. So literary reform was the precursor of the cultural movement, the political movement, and the social movement. At the time of Germany's fifteenth-century religious movement (actually, a minor part of Europe's great social and political movement, which borrowed the outer clothing of religion), Martin Luther's translation of the Bible into spoken German paved the way for Germany's new literary movement. The same thing happened after the importation into China of Buddhist culture in the Wei [220-265] and Jin [265-420] dynasties, when a group of intelligent monks headed by Kumarajiva[46] pioneered translation literature and, by their unprecedented endeavour, cleared away the fog of the classical written language. In the May Fourth Movement, Mr Duxiu and others resolutely took upon themselves the task of reforming written Chinese, and thereby simply met the new demands that had arisen in China at that time. Although some people in those days considered it somewhat extreme to wield one's pen furiously and declare war on the old literature, actually and ideologically this sort of reform was a movement for revolution. When revolutionaries storm the imperial palace to destroy the *ancien régime*, audacity and ruthlessness are indispensable. Of course, one must not forget in discussing China's new literary movement the pioneering achievements of Mr Liang Rengong,[47] who

43. Actually, the main project of the literary movement was to create new forms of written Chinese rather than a new literature as such.
44. The revolution under Sun Yat-sen that overthrew the Qing dynasty and inaugurated the Chinese Republic.
45. The actual name of this journal was *Anhui suhua bao* (also meaning "Anhui Vernacular Magazine"), not *Anhui baihua bao*; it was published in 1904.
46. Kumarajiva, born in Central Asia to an Indian father, was captured by a Chinese expedition around 382 and taken to China, where he headed a major project to translate Buddhist scriptures into Chinese.
47. I.e., Liang Qichao.

after the Reform Movement of 1898 courageously wrote articles using Europeanised sentence constructions, strove to import the whole range of Japanese and Western scientific and cultural names and technical terms, and transplanted Japanese and Western style into Chinese literature; in the initial stages of China's new literary movement, he played an undeniably enlightening and pioneering role. But only Chen Duxiu and Hu Shizhi laid the foundations on a grand scale for the founding of a new literary universe. Moreover, Hu Shizhi received his professorial appointment at Beijing University due to the strenuous efforts of Chen Duxiu. That gives us some idea of Mr Duxiu's position in China's new literary movement.

Third, I wish to look at Mr Duxiu the man. It is well-known that thinkers or writers who want in the course of their life's struggle to maintain an absolute balance between academic creation and moral integrity must have the determination and courage to sacrifice themselves for the truth, a spirit that manifests itself above all in the ability to endure poverty and hardship. Thirty years ago, Mr Duxiu, baggage and umbrella slung across his shoulder, scoured north and south of the rivers Yangtse and Huai in search of revolutionary comrades to prepare to overthrow the Qing and establish a republic. Wang Mengzou,[48] an old and lifelong friend of Mr Duxiu, had opened a bookshop in Wuhu and secretly maintained relations with the revolutionaries. One day, Mr Duxiu turned up, bag in one hand and umbrella in the other. Mr Wang said, "All I have to eat here are two meals of gruel a day, life's really hard." "Two meals of gruel a day? That's great," replied Mr Duxiu, drily. So he stayed on, and spent every day in the room above the bookshop editing the *Anhui Vernacular Magazine* and making propaganda for the revolution; that was in the thirtieth year [i.e., 1904] of the Guangxu reign [1875-1908]. After the defeat of the second revolution (against Yuan [Shikai]),[49] Mr Bo Liewu[50] withdrew from Anqing,[51] so Mr Duxiu fled to Shanghai, where he lived in Yuyang Terrace, in the French Settlement; there he edited the early *Qingnian* ["Youth"] (the forerunner of *Xin qingnian*). He was still eating two meals of gruel a day, but he never once tried to borrow money from his friends; for

48. Wang Mengzou (Wang Meng-tsou) (1877-1953) was a publisher and a supporter of all progressive movements in China since the beginning of the century.
49. In 1913, Sun Yat-sen, leader of the Guomindang and architect of the destruction of the Qing dynasty, tried to regroup his revolutionary supporters to overthrow the increasingly dictatorial regime of Yuan Shikai, president of the new republic. This "second revolution" was quickly defeated.
50. Another name of Bo Wenwei, the first revolutionary governor of Anhui province.
51. The capital at the time of Anhui province, where Bo Liewu was governor.

in matters of taking money from or giving it to others, he was extremely circumspect and stringent. As for Mr Duxiu's second virtue, I would say that he was wholly indifferent to death. I remember that after the defeat of the second revolution, when he was fleeing from Anqing to Wuhu, he was captured by troops of the Wuhu garrison. This military man [the commander of the garrison] had originally stood alongside Bo Liewu under the banner of opposition to Yuan Shikai, but for some reason he'd fallen out with Bo; now he was venting his anger on Mr Duxiu. He'd already issued a notice announcing that Mr Duxiu would be shot. Mr Duxiu coolly urged him, "If you're going to shoot me, then get on with it." The execution was averted at the last moment through the strenuous efforts of Mr Duxiu's friends Liu Shuya, Fan Hongyan, and Zhang Zigang,[52] who intervened to secure his release. Later, [in 1932,] after Mr Duxiu had been arrested in Shanghai by the Guomindang government, he fell soundly asleep while under police escort on the way to Nanjing, and did not wake until the train arrived in Nanjing the following morning, as if it were simply a day like any other.[53] This calm composure and fearlessness in the face of mortal danger were typical of the man. Unless one understands this moral essence of Mr Duxiu, one will fail to understand his entire personality and the worth of his legacy to us in the field of Chinese cultural history. Finally, I solemnly repeat: We must absolutely avoid [distorting a person's achievements, by either] exaggerating or belittling [them].

52. A group of influential people in Wuhu at that time.
53. Chen had been arrested on October 15, 1932, together with the entire Trotskyist leadership then still at large, in Shanghai's International Settlement, whence he was extradited to the Chinese authorities; this was his fourth (and last) arrest. It was widely believed at the time that he would be sentenced to death by the court in Nanjing, where he was sent to stand trial. The Guomindang organised a big propaganda campaign to call for his execution. At his trial, Chen calmly justified working for the overthrow of the Guomindang Government, on the grounds that the government had failed to defend China against Japanese aggression and had suppressed basic rights and freedoms. "I rebelled not against the nation but against the Guomindang," he told the court. Liberals and other non-Communist radicals flocked to Chen's support. Probably as a result, he was sentenced not to death but to thirteen years in prison.

Appendix 5

THE STRUGGLE WITH CHEN DU-HSIU [CHEN DUXIU][54]

Ming-yuen Wang[55]

This assessment of Chen Duxiu is excerpted from a document of the International- ist Group of Chinese Trotskyists published in The New International, *the journal of Max Shachtman's Workers Party, a Trotskyist organisation in the USA, in February 1948. The document deals mainly with the problem of policy in the Sino-Japanese War and the subsequent civil war between the Guomindang and the Communist Party, but it begins with this review of the politics of Chen Duxiu at his life's end. After the Japanese attack on the US fleet at Pearl Harbor in December 1941 and the start of the Pacific War, the Trotskyists' Communist League of China had split into a majority, the Douzheng ("Struggle") Group, so called after the title of its paper, led by Peng Shuzhi, and the minority Interna- tionalist Group under Wang Fanxi and Zheng Chaolin. A document of the majority Struggle Group had been published in the Socialist Workers Party's* Fourth International *of July-August 1947; it is referred to below as the Report.*

The Report begins with a description of the struggle carried on between the Chinese Trotskyist organization and Chen Du-hsiu. It attempts to describe the relations which existed between the Chinese Old Man and the revolution- ists of the 1925–27 generation.[56] The Report says of Chen Du-hsiu: "He turned his back upon our League almost immediately after he left prison" and "declared in a letter to one of our old comrades in Shanghai that he had decided to combat damned Bolshevism to the very end of his life!"

Such a description is oversimplified, therefore incorrect. Chen Du-hsiu, "the father of Chinese communism," the general secretary of the Chinese Commu- nist Party from its very inception until August 1927, the No. 1 leader of the Chinese revolution of 1925–27, who became a Trotskyist after the debacle of the revolution, became one of the founders and leaders of the Chinese

---

54. Source: M. Y. Wang, "Chinese Trotskyism in the War," *The New International*, February 1948, pp. 58–62.
55. I.e., Wang Fanxi.
56. The Report described the leaders of the Internationalist Group as "comrades who belong to the 1925–27 generation".

Trotskyist movement, served four years in a Kuomintang prison while remaining a staunch Trotskyist – Chen Du-hsiu did break with Bolshevism during the Second World War. But this break did not take place "immediately" and it was not final.

During the period from the beginning of the anti-Japanese war down to the outbreak of the Second World War, he held the position that the Chinese Trotskyists could do nothing else than support the anti-Japanese war unconditionally. In his opinion it was quite out of the question to speak of revolution during the war or of transforming the war into a revolution. But as usual with him, Chen Du-hsiu did not present this position as a matter of principle but rather empirically and tactically. He justified his position in the following manner: We must at present support the war; as for this revolution, let's speak of it later. You can see from this that Chen Du-hsiu's position was false; but it was neither final nor systematic.

Chen's Break with the Movement

In 1939, one year after the beginning of the Sino-Japanese War, in order to acquaint himself with the position of the Chinese Old Man, Trotsky asked Comrade Li Fu-jen [Li Furen] to make an inquiry of him. Chen Du-hsiu wrote a statement in answer which was given to Trotsky by Li Fu-jen. After reading Chen Du-hsiu's statement Trotsky wrote Comrade Li as follows: "I am extremely glad to know that our friend remained our friend politically, although there are some *possible* divergences existing between us; but right now I cannot judge these *possible* divergences with necessary precision.... However, I consider that what he expressed is essentially correct." (Trotsky's letter to Li Fu-jen, retranslated from the Chinese, March 11, 1939.)[57]

Chen Du-hsiu's position moved further away from that of the Trotskyists after the signing of the German-Soviet Pact [in August 1939] and the outbreak of war in Europe. He held that we should support the democracies versus the fascist and Russian "imperialisms." He was of the opinion that in order to facilitate the victory of the democracies in the war, the Indians should for the time being put a stop to their nationalist movement.

It goes without saying that this is the same as the position that was held by Plekhanov, Guesde & Co. during the First World War and that was held by the Second International, and by the Third International after the outbreak

---

57. See Appendix 2 for the full text of Trotsky's letter.

of the German-Soviet war, during the last slaughter of mankind. Needless to say, such a position meant a complete break with Trotskyism.

But, as we have said and as Trotsky had correctly observed, Chen Du-hsiu was not a theoretician of Plekhanov's type but a revolutionist à la Lassalle. Lacking profound theoretical training, his action was always directed by impressions, his opinions were changeable and fallible; but at the same time and for the same reason he was often able to make bold corrections of his mistakes.

The over-thirty-years' history of Chen Du-hsiu's revolutionary activity was replete with such conflicts and mistakes. One's defects sometimes become one's merit. It was partially because of this "defect," we believe, that Chen Du-hsiu was able to complete his evolution from a democrat to a communist and from a communist in general to a Trotskyist, in the brief period of seven or eight years.

We may speculate whether, if Chen had not died, he would have devoted the remaining years of his life to the cause of the Fourth International. We cannot give a definite answer to this question. That is why we also said that his break with Trotskyism could not be considered as final.

Appendix 6

ON CHEN DUXIU'S "LAST VIEWS"[58]

Shuang Shan[59]

Between 1936 and 1938 and again in late 1939 or early 1940, the Trotskyist Wang Fanxi had a vigorous exchange of views with Chen Duxiu on the issue of democracy. Sometime in 1936 Chen Duxiu, then in prison, smuggled out an article on democracy to the Trotskyists in Shanghai, where Wang published it in Huohua ("Spark") together with his own critical comments. Three or four years later, Wang again discussed this same question with Chen, by then in Sichuan, in letters that he wrote to him from Shanghai. This volume contains Chen's correspondence with Wang and others who wrote to Chen in similar vein.

Chen's view, expressed in his last letters and articles, that Lenin had fathered Stalinism, and Chen's rejection of dictatorship of any sort, revolutionary or counterrevolutionary, alienated his Trotskyist comrades, who believed (as orthodox Leninists) in a dictatorship of the workers. Wang's replies to Chen in Spark and the letters he wrote to him before Chen died have apparently been lost, but in an article written in Macau in 1957, Wang summarised in seven points positions derived from those that he had developed in his last exchanges with Chen. Wang's seven theses show that far from rejecting Chen's criticism outright, he strove to incorporate its insights into his own political thinking and to reconcile the idea of checks and balances, political pluralism, and democratic rights with the need for violent revolution and proletarian dictatorship.

🌏

1. Under present historical conditions, if the proletariat through its political party aims to overthrow the political and economic rule of the bourgeoisie, it must carry out a violent revolution and set up a dictatorship to expropriate the expropriators. So in nine cases out of ten it is bound to destroy the bourgeoisie's traditional means of rule – the parliamentary system. To com-

58. Source: Shuang Shan, "Cong Chen Duxiude 'zuihou yijian' shuoqi" ("On Chen Duxiu's 'Last Views'"), in *Sixiang wenti* ("Some ideological questions"), Hongkong: N. p., 1957, pp. 5–6.
59. I.e., Wang Fanxi.

plete such a transformation "peacefully", through parliament, is practically if not absolutely impossible.

2. A proletarian dictatorship set up in such a way neither must nor should destroy the various democratic rights – including habeus corpus; freedom of speech, the press, assembly, and association; the right to strike; etc., etc. – already won by the people under the bourgeois democratic system.

3. The organs of the dictatorship elected by the entire toiling people should be under the thorough-going supervision of the electors and recallable by them at all times; and the power of the dictatorship should not be concentrated in one body but should be spread across several structures so that there is a system of checks and balances to prevent the emergence of an autocracy or monocracy.

4. Opposition parties should be allowed to exist under the dictatorship as long as they support the revolution. Whether or not they meet this condition should be decided by the workers and peasants in free ballot.

5. Opposition factions must be tolerated within the party of the proletariat. Under no circumstances must organisational sanctions, secret service measures, or incriminatory sanctions be used to deal with dissidents; under no circumstances must thought be made a crime.

6. Under no circumstances must proletarian dictatorship become the dictatorship of a single party. Workers' parties organised by part of the working class and the intelligentsia must under no circumstances replace the political power democratically elected by the toilers as a whole. There must be an end to the present system in the Communist countries, where government is a facade behind which secretaries of the party branches assume direct command. The ruling party's strategic policies must first be discussed and approved by an empowered parliament (or soviet) that includes opposition parties and factions, and only then should they be implemented by government; and their implementation must continue to be supervised by parliament.

7. Finally, ... since political democracy is actually a reflection of economic democracy and no political democracy is possible under a system of absolutely centralised economic control,... to create the material base for socialist democracy a system of divided power and self-management within the overall planned economy is essential.

All these points are not in themselves enough to save a revolutionary power from bureaucratic degeneration; but since they are not plucked from the void but rooted in bloody experience, they should – if formulated with sufficient clarity – (a) help workers and peasants in countries that have had revolutions to win their anti-bureaucratic struggle when the conditions for the democratisation of the dictatorial state have further ripened; and (b) enable new revolutionary states from the very outset to avoid bureaucratic poisoning.

Appendix 7

CHEN DUXIU, FOUNDER OF CHINESE COMMUNISM[60]

Wang Fanxi

To many younger Chinese socialists, the name Chen Duxiu means little, and to most socialists outside China, it means nothing at all. Of China's main Communist leaders, only Mao, Zhou Enlai, Liu Shaoqi, and a handful of others have won fame in the outside world. How could Chen, a nonentity, stand alongside these great leaders? But in truth, Chen was anything but a nonentity in the history of the Chinese Revolution. If judged not just by what he achieved directly but by his influence over an entire historical period, he ranks not only above Zhou and Liu, but even above Mao himself.

In 1936, in conversation with Edgar Snow, Zhou and Mao frankly acknowledged Chen's influence on them, and Snow reported their remarks in his classic *Red Star Over China*. But Zhou and Mao apparently had second thoughts, for the Chinese translation of Snow's book was withdrawn from circulation in the spring of 1938. Zhou had told Snow: "Before going to France, I read translations of the *Communist Manifesto*; Kautsky's *Class Struggle*; and *The October Revolution*. These books were published under the auspices of *Xin qingnian*, which was published by Ch'en Tu-hsiu [Chen Duxiu]. I also personally met Ch'en Tu-hsiu as well as Li Ta-chao [Li Dazhao] – who were to become founders of the Chinese Communist Party." Mao Zedong said: "I went to Shanghai for the second time in 1919. There once more I saw Ch'en Tu-hsiu. I had first met him in Peking [Beijing], when I was at Peking National University, and he had influenced me perhaps more than anyone else." So Mao was Chen's pupil, not just before the Party was founded, but for a long time afterwards, too.

Chen Duxiu was born on October 8, 1879, thirty-five years after the Opium War and fifteen years after the defeat of the Taiping Rebellion. Outer pressure and inner dissension had already shaken the Qing dynasty to its foundations. The corruption and incompetence of the imperial system and

60. This assessment of Chen first appeared in a slightly different form in Gregor Benton, ed., *Wild Lilies: Poisonous Weeds. Dissident Voices from People's China*, London: Pluto Press, 1982, pp. 157-167.

the growing Western threat had woken many Chinese intellectuals to the need for reform. So when Chen Duxiu was born, China was already in the first stages of political ferment and change.

But Chen was brought up in a strictly traditional way. Born into an Anhui gentry family, he lost his father in the first months of his life, and was raised and educated by his grandfather and his elder brother. The latter were both classical Confucianists, and they set out to train the young Duxiu for the imperial examinations, which were the sole path to bureaucratic office under the Qing.

Chen had no liking for the Confucian classics and even less liking for the *bagu* or eight-legged essay, a form of composition in which examination candidates were required to excel. However, to please his grandfather and his mother, he took the first exam at the age of seventeen and came top of the list with a *xiucai* degree.[61] The following year, in 1897, he went to Nanjing to take part in the triennial examination for the degree of *juren*. As a result of his experiences there, he lost interest once and for all in the imperial examinations and, more importantly, began to question the soundness of China's basic institutions. He vividly described his feelings in his unfinished autobiography. One candidate, a fat man from Xuzhou, who paced up and down the examination pen naked but for a pair of broken sandals, chanting his favourite *bagu*, made a particularly deep impression on Chen.

> I could not take my eyes off him. As I watched, I fell to thinking about the whole strange business of the examination system, and then I began to think about how much my country and its people would suffer once these brutes achieved positions of power. Finally, I began to doubt the whole system of selecting talent through examination. It was like a circus of monkeys and bears, repeated every so many years. But was the examination system an exception, or were not China's other institutions equally rotten? I ended up agreeing with the criticisms raised in the newspaper *Shiwu* ["Contemporary Events"], and I switched my allegiance from the examination system to the reformist party of Kang Youwei[62] and Liang Qichao. And so an hour or two of pondering decided the course of my life for the next dozen years.

The Kang-Liang reform movement was considered very radical when Chen Duxiu joined it. It called for the replacement of the absolute monarchy by a

61. The first degree, gained at county level, in the imperial examinations under the Ming and Qing dynasties.
62. Kang Youwei (K'ang Yu-wei) (1858-1927) was leader of the reform movement that culminated in the short-lived Hundred Days Reform of 1898 and was a prominent scholar of the New Text School of the Confucian classics.

constitutional monarchy, and it proposed a series of reforms to change China. But just a year later, in 1898, the reformists suffered a crushing defeat, and in 1900 the Qing rulers were humiliated by eight foreign powers during the Yihetuan (or Boxer) upheavals. Chen's outlook on life and politics became more and more radical under the impact of these events. In 1904, in Anhui, he published *Suhua bao* ["Vernacular magazine"], a newspaper written in vernacular Chinese. In 1908, he went to Shanghai, where he joined an underground terrorist group and learned how to make bombs. By now, his political views had already left Kang and Liang way behind, and he was advocating the overthrow of the Qing dynasty by force.

Even before the fall of the Qing in 1911, Chen was arrested for his political activities in Anhui. After his release, he was driven into exile in Japan. There he collaborated with Sun Yat-sen, founder of the Guomindang and chief architect of the Qing's overthrow, but he did not join Sun's organisation. On his return to China during the 1911 Revolution, Chen became political director of the revolutionary army in Anhui. But after the Nationalists compromised with Yuan Shikai, representative of the *ancien régime*, he was once again forced into exile in Japan, where he published a revolutionary newspaper. Returning to China in 1915, he founded the journal *Qingnian* ("Youth") in Shanghai, renamed *Xin qingnian* the following year. *Xin qingnian* played a major role in the further unfolding of the Chinese Revolution. In 1917, *Xin qingnian*'s editorial board moved north to Beijing, where Chen was invited to become Dean of Letters at Beijing National University, China's highest and most progressive institution. Here were gathered many of China's best scholars, including Li Dazhao,[63] a founder and early martyr of the Chinese Communist Party; Dr Hu Shi, the philosopher; Lu Xun,[64] the essayist; Qian Xuantong, the historian; and Zhou Zuoren,[65] the essayist. With their help and that of some students, *Xin qingnian* quickly gained in circulation and influence.

In any case, circumstances favoured its rapid growth. The war in Europe had temporarily loosened the West's economic grip on China, so that a national bourgeoisie was born, and, with it, a modern working class. At the same time, revolution was brewing in Russia, and in 1917 the Bolsheviks took

63. Li Dazhao (Li Ta-chao) (1889-1927) was one of the founders of the Chinese Communist Party, second only to Chen Duxiu. He was executed in Beijing in 1927.
64. Lu Xun (Lu Hsün) (1881-1936), modern China's best-known novelist, essayist, and critic, was known as "China's Gorky". His original name was Zhou Shuren.
65. Zhou Zuoren (Chou Tso-jen) (1885-1968), a main contributor to Chen Duxiu's *Xin qingnian*, introduced Japanese and Eastern European literature into China. He was the brother of Lu Xun.

power in a revolution that decisively influenced modern China's course. Many ideological and social movements sprang up throughout the world, and especially in Europe, at the end of the war. Thus encouraged, some Chinese intellectuals began to search more earnestly than ever for new solutions to the problems that China had faced ever since being dragged into the world's eddy by Western businessmen and soldiers. At the same time, these social and political developments gave the intellectuals a ready-made audience of tens of thousands, and a firm social base on which to realise their ideals.

Xin qingnian did not begin as a directly political publication. In the early days, it campaigned on two main fronts: against China's traditional ethics and social practices; and against classical Chinese, which was still used for most written communication. The campaign against traditional ethics was known as the New Thought Movement, and the campaign against classical Chinese was known as the Literary Revolution. On the first front, *Xin qingnian*, especially Chen Duxiu, took Confucius as the main target. Confucianism had dominated China for over two millennia, and was the ideological mainstay of the whole reactionary system. For Chen and his comrades, China's backwardness was due above all to its ossification under Confucian teaching; they believed that there could be no social progress until the Chinese people was freed from the Confucian grip. The Literary Revolution was closely linked to this struggle against Confucianism. Classical Chinese, based on the spoken language of more than one thousand years ago, differed radically from modern spoken Chinese. So until it was replaced by a written form based on modern spoken Chinese, mass illiteracy would remain and progressive intellectuals would never be able to waken the people. This was not the first time that Chen had called for language reform. As early as 1904 he had published a newspaper with articles in the vernacular. But it was only now that the conditions for a literary revolution had fully ripened. Now, despite stiff opposition from the literati, daily speech finally won out, and living Chinese replaced dead Chinese as the official means of communication.

Yet Chen Duxiu's main contribution to the New Thought Movement and the Literary Revolution lay less in his constructive achievement than in his destructive energy: in his dauntless urge to discredit, criticise, and destroy everything traditional. He was among the greatest iconoclasts in the history of human thought; and, like all iconoclasts and pioneers, he worked not with a scalpel but with a bulldozer. For him, the main thing was to pull down the dilapidated house of the past, and this he did to devastating effect. But for a long time he had only the vaguest idea of what sort of house to put in its place, except that it must be in the Western style. So during the first four years of *Xin qingnian*, Chen Duxiu should properly be called a Westerniser or a radical bourgeois democrat. He admired almost everything Western, especially great events and people from the past three centuries of European history; he cited them enthusiastically in his writings, comparing them with events and people from the Chinese past. Great names like Francis Bacon, Jean-Jacques Rousseau, Auguste Comte, Charles Darwin, Louis Pasteur, Victor Hugo, Emile Zola, Kant, Hegel, Goethe, Dickens, and even Oscar Wilde he introduced indiscriminately as models for Chinese youth to admire and emulate. But he did not know these people well, nor did he have a sound grasp of Western thought. He mastered no European language, so he acquired all his new knowledge through Japanese translations; and his Japanese was not good either. The result was that all he learned from the West were a few broad concepts such as humanism, democracy, individualism, and scientific method. From these, he singled out democracy and science as the two surgeons capable of saving China.

The October Revolution of 1917 had an enormous effect on Chen's thinking, but it was not until later that Chen definitively embraced Marxism and concluded that China would never become modernised unless the Chinese, like the Bolsheviks, carried out an economic as well as a political revolution.

It was above all May Fourth that precipitated this change in Chen's thinking. On May 4, 1919, a student movement broke out in Beijing and spread to all China's major cities. This movement was in protest against the decision of the Paris Peace Conference to transfer German concessions in China to Japan, and against the Beijing government for acting as Japan's tool. May Fourth happened under the direct influence of Chen's *Xin qingnian* journal. It was *Xin qingnian*'s first victory, but also its first big test. May Fourth quickly split the *Xin qingnian* leaders into two competing camps. For some time, a process of differentiation had been going on among the journal's main supporters. Now, this process quickened. Chen Duxiu and Li Dazhao went further to the left and plunged into revolutionary work, while Hu Shi and others moved further to the right under the pretext of "retreating to the study".

As a leader of May Fourth and its chief inspirer, Chen Duxiu was the main target for government repression at the end of it. In June, he was seized and gaoled for three months. After his release, he left Beijing University for good, and began a critical review of the doctrines that he had earlier indiscriminately adopted. In September 1920, he declared himself a Marxist.

Now that he had committed himself wholly to the revolution, he began to work toward the establishment of a Communist Party in China. In August 1920, he set up a Socialist Youth Corps in Shanghai. At the same time, Marxist Study Groups were organised in big cities throughout China. In July 1921, the Chinese Communist Party held its First National Congress in Shanghai. Chen was elected General Secretary, and the following year he represented the Party at the Fourth Congress of the Communist International in Moscow. He was reelected leader at the following four Party Congresses; he led the Party during the Revolution of 1925-27.

The Revolution of 1925-27 has been called a tragedy by some historians, and it certainly ended in tragic defeats. What was Chen's role in that tragedy? There are various answers to this question, which has been the subject of much heated controversy. The view of the Communist International and (until recently) of the Chinese Communist Party was that Chen was an opportunist and a bungler whose wrong policy led the revolution to defeat. According to this view, the main if not the exclusive blame for the defeat was Chen Duxiu's. But not everyone agrees with this assessment. Some of Chen's fellow-revolutionaries and many scholars believe that Chen's mistake was to be too faithful to the directives of the Comintern, which was then controlled by Stalin and Bukharin, and that he was merely Stalin's scapegoat. My own experience of the events of 1925-27, and my later reflections on them, led me too to this conclusion.

Chen Duxiu was dismissed as Party leader at the August 7 (1927) Emergency Conference of the Central Committee. He was succeeded by Qu Qiubai, who under Moscow's orders switched to an adventurist line culminating in the disastrous Guangzhou [Canton] Insurrection of December 1927. In retirement, Chen wrote several letters to the Party warning against putschism and demanding a critical review of policy, but this merely widened the gap between him and the new leaders.

In late 1929, Chen could acquaint himself with the Russian Left Opposition's views on China through documents brought back to China by Communists who had studied in Moscow. Until then, Chen had no true understanding of the differences between Trotsky and Stalin on the Chinese Revolution. These documents opened up a new field of vision for him, and helped dispel doubts that had vexed him for years. He soon went over to the positions of the Left Opposition, and wrote to the Party leaders demanding that the issues in the Chinese Revolution should be put up for discussion in the Party and in the entire world Communist movement. He was promptly expelled as a result; in response, he wrote his famous "Open Letter to all Comrades" of December 10, 1929, and put his name to the statement "Our Political Views" signed by eighty-one veteran Party members. Needless to say, all these people were expelled from the Party. A few months later, in February 1930, Stalin tried to "win Chen Duxiu back" by inviting him to Moscow. Chen turned down the invitation, thus severing all ties with the Party he had founded nine years earlier.

Chen then organised his followers into a Left Opposition and published the newspaper *Wuchanzhe* ["Proletarian"]. In May 1931, this organisation merged with three other Trotskyist groups to form the Chinese section of the International of Bolshevik-Leninists, of which Chen was elected General Secretary. But in October 1932, Chen was arrested and put before the Nanjing Military Tribunal, where he faced the death sentence. In court, he behaved every inch like a revolutionary leader; from the dock, he denounced the Guomindang's regime of terror. His arrest and trial led to a nationwide campaign to free him. As a result, he was spared the death penalty and given a thirteen-year gaol sentence instead.

Chen stayed in prison until shortly after the outbreak of the Sino-Japanese War in 1937, when he was freed along with other political prisoners, but he was still kept under strict watch, and this prevented him from doing revolutionary work. After a brief stay in Wuhan, he was compelled to stay in a small town near Chongqing in Sichuan province, where the Guomindang had its wartime capital. His health had worsened in prison, and on May 27, 1942, he died of heart sickness and phlebitis, aged sixty-four.

Chen spent his last years in great poverty, bad health, and isolation. Nevertheless, the Guomindang and the Communist Party persecuted him to the end. In the summer of 1938, the Communist Party began a strident slander campaign against him. This campaign was directed by Wang Ming, Stalin's chief representative in China. Wang Ming accused Chen of "collaborating with the Japanese imperialists". At the same time, the Guomindang prohibited Chen from resuming his literary activities. All he could do during those hard times was to think and to exchange opinions by letter with a few old friends. After his death, these letters and a few articles from the years 1940-42 were compiled by one of his former pupils, He Zishen, and published in Shanghai in 1948. In 1949, Dr Hu Shi, once an old friend of Chen's but later a staunch supporter of Chiang Kai-shek, reprinted this collection of writings in Taiwan, and wrote an introduction to it in which he welcomed Chen's ideas as those of a "prodigal returned". As for the Chinese Communist Party, it regarded Chen as a renegade, and even some Trotskyists thought the same, although for different reasons. So what was Chen's new position, and did it represent his final reconciliation with bourgeois thought?

The main themes of Chen's last letters and articles were as follows. First, no revolutions would break out during the war, and only if the Allies defeated the Axis would revolutionary crises happen. Socialists throughout the world were therefore duty-bound to support the democratic Allies against the Fascist Axis. Second, there is no essential difference between bourgeois and proletarian democracy, but only a difference of degree. Proletarian democracy is therefore an extension rather than a negation of bourgeois democracy, and it is wrong to say that bourgeois democracy is historically superseded. Third, capitalism is the root of war, which only world revolution can end. Fourth, the struggle for national liberation is interlinked with proletarian revolution in the advanced countries, and the forces behind these two struggles make socialist revolution together. Fifth, the Soviet Union under Lenin was qualitatively different from the Soviet Union under Stalin. The former was socialist, the latter was not. (Chen died before he could elaborate on what kind of regime the Soviet Union under Stalin had become.) Sixth, although Lenin's regime was not like Stalin's, Lenin was partly to blame for Stalin's crimes, since it was he who had counterposed proletarian dictatorship to democracy in general. Seventh, a true socialist revolution is one in which democracy -or, more exactly, democratic rights – are respected and extended.

Chen's thinking had changed greatly during the early war years, but his views, however muddled, still fell far short of a reconciliation with his old enemy, the bourgeoisie. Instead, they represented a return by Chen in his old age to the positions he had held as a young man. It is interesting to ask why this happened, especially since in my experience it is not uncommon for intellectuals in backward countries to revert in this way to the ideas of their youth.

China's isolation was broken down by guns and ships. China's "modernisation" stemmed not from gradual change based on evolutions within its own society, but from outside pressures. Development of this sort is inevitably by leaps and bounds, and is condensed and telescoped. In China, the transition from democratic radicalism to the founding of a modern socialist movement took some twenty years. In Britain and France, the same process took several centuries, and in Russia it took several scores of years.

Moreover, China's progress from democratic agitation to full-blown Communism took place in one and the same person: Chen Duxiu. Chen was China's Belinsky, Chernyshevsky, Plekhanov, and Lenin rolled into one. True, he reached the stature of none of these great Russians, but he traversed the entire gamut of their thinking, from the first awakening of individualism to the struggle for socialist collectivism. Thus, Chen embodies what Russian Marxists referred to as combined development. However, combined development is both a privilege and a curse. It explains not only Chen's merits but also his faults. Chen rapidly and boldly assimilated an impressive list of isms, but in none did he reach real depth. In his teens, he became a "left-wing Confucianist"; in his twenties, he was intoxicated by Western democracy; in his thirties, he criticised Confucianism; and at 41, he became a Marxist. Inevitably, he retained elements of older ideologies among the new ones, as he raced from one ism to the next. And by the time that he embraced Marxism, he had reached an age where new thinking rarely sinks deep into the soul. So it is understandable that, in the last years of his life, Chen returned in part to his intellectual first love, "pure" democracy.

Other factors, too, disposed Chen to look favourably on democracy. Above all, he was appalled by the degeneration of the Stalinist regime in the Soviet Union. It was the Moscow trials that initially led him to rethink the Leninist view of bourgeois democracy.

How, then, should one appraise Chen's life? Despite his political failures and his intellectual limitations, Chen was not only modern China's bravest thinker but one of history's great revolutionaries, because of both his leading role in the Chinese Revolution and his personal indomitability. He did not hesitate to give up a brilliant career for the uncertain and hard life of a revolutionary. He heroically bore the loss of his family and his two sons (murdered by the Guomindang in 1927 and 1928). He stuck to his beliefs under the threat of imprisonment and death. And during the last years of his life, when he was gravely ill and desperately poor, he refused to accept money offered him by the Guomindang through one of his old friends. All this shows that Chen was a man of revolutionary mettle; his memory remains that of a great revolutionary. Another appraisal of Chen is that he was "an oppositionist for life to any established authority", and Chen himself liked this description of his career.

Appendix 8

CHEN DUXIU AND THE TROTSKYISTS[66]

Zheng Chaolin

This appendix comprises the concluding section of a special study by the veteran Trotskyist Zheng Chaolin (arrested by the Shanghai political police in 1952 and finally freed in 1979, aged 78) on Chen Duxiu's relationship to Trotskyism; the study was commissioned by Party historians to supplement their planned publication of Zheng's memoirs, which had been completed (but not published) in 1945 and was unearthed from a government vault in 1979, shortly after Zheng's release from gaol. In 1986, after sitting for several years on the manuscript of the memoirs and the newly commissioned supplement, Chinese Communist officials finally authorised their publication, in an edition restricted to privileged categories of officials and researchers. On December 11, 1987, Zheng explained in a postscript to the English translation of his memoirs the circumstances under which he had composed the study on Chen Duxiu: "I wrote the appendix 'Chen Duxiu and the Trotskyists' at the invitation of a certain research institute in 1980, shortly after I had regained my freedom. At the time, public opinion tended to make a distinction between Chen Duxiu and the Trotskyists. People said that Chen Duxiu was a good man whose good name should be restored, but they made no evaluation of the Trotskyists. So the aim of this long article is to show that Chen Duxiu and the Trotskyists cannot be dealt with separately."[67]

❧

Was or was not Chen Duxiu a Trotskyist? This is one of the hardest questions currently facing students of contemporary Chinese history and people who wish to study and grasp the present political situation in China. Chen's role in Chinese and world history can never be rubbed out. The old slanders against him cannot be upheld.

Just think of the picture of Chen Duxiu painted by several generations of political commentators! An opportunist who buried the Great Revolution,

---

66. Excerpted from Zheng Chaolin, "Chen Duxiu and the Trotskyists," pp. 197–202.
67. Quoted in Benton, *China's Urban Revolutionaries*, p. 250.

a renegade, a national traitor, a paid agent of the Guomindang, a counterrevolutionary, and so on. The founder of the Chinese Communist Party, elected its top leader at five successive congresses, was that sort of man? Some people even go so far as to claim that the leader of the May Fourth Movement of 1919 was not Chen Duxiu but someone else.[68]

Things began to change only in 1979, which was Chen's hundredth birthday and the sixtieth anniversary of May Fourth, after which the press began to recognise Chen's role in leading it. Around July 1 and October 1[69] of that year, the press also started to recognise Chen's role in founding the Chinese Communist Party. The Museum of the Revolution in Beijing displayed his picture and the taboo on discussing the relationship between the Comintern and the Chinese Communist Party was broken. Historians began to reach new conclusions that were more in accordance with the facts. Articles began to appear in the open and the internal press[70] showing that when Chen Duxiu said in 1923 that China's bourgeois revolution would be led by the bourgeoisie, he was simply representing the Comintern's point of view; and that when in 1926 and 1927 the Chinese Communist Party was pursuing an opportunist line, it was also following Comintern directives. Later, during the War of Resistance to Japan, an article appeared in *Xinhua ribao* ["New China Daily"] accusing Chen Duxiu and Luo Han of coming to an agreement through Tang Youren with Japanese intelligence by which they would be paid $300 a month: but now evidence has been produced to reveal this as a political calumny. In the past, people used to say that Chen's three letters to the Central Committee of the Chinese Communist Party about the Chinese Eastern Railway Incident proved that he had gone over to the counterrevolution, but now others are saying that in this controversy the Central Committee was wrong and Chen was right. As for the charge that he capitulated to the Guomindang, became an agent, and took money from Chiang Kai-shek, many, many people have now produced evidence to rebut it.

Finally, there is the question of the Trotskyists. The Comintern taboo has already been broken; but the taboo on Trotskyism remains, and people carry on repeating – as they have been doing for decades now – that the international Trotskyists and the Chinese Trotskyists are counterrevolutionaries. So how

68. For many years, the pretence was maintained in China that the May Fourth Movement was led by Li Dazhao and Lu Xun.
69. The anniversaries of the founding of the Party (in 1921) and of the People's Republic (in 1949).
70. The internal or *neibu* press is accessible only to privileged categories of people.

come Chen Duxiu, leader of May Fourth and founder of the Chinese Communist Party, got mixed up with this counterrevolutionary political organisation?

Some people say that he was influenced only intellectually by Trotsky, and that he didn't join the Trotskyist organisation.

Some people say that he joined the Trotskyist organisation but broke with it after the Guomindang arrested him.

Some people say that after his release from the Guomindang gaol he declared that he was not a Trotskyist, i.e., that he broke with the Trotskyist organisation, and that after that there is no evidence that he had anything more to do with the Trotskyists.

Some people say that when he joined the Trotskyist organisation the Trotskyist question was still a contradiction among the people,[71] and that by the time the Trotskyists had become a bunch of murderers and foreign spies he had already broken with them.

Some people say that he gave up his Trotskyist ideas a few years before he died.

And so on.

Naturally, there are also people who know full well that the Trotskyists are anything but counterrevolutionary and that Chen Duxiu's conversion to Trotskyism and his membership of the Trotskyist organisation were an organic outcome of his entire intellectual development. But they still don't dare say so in public.

In my view, there is no longer any need for me today to defend Chen Duxiu against the charge that he was an "opportunist", that he was to blame for the defeat of the revolution, or that he was a "counterrevolutionary", a "renegade", an "agent", a "running dog of the Guomindang", and a "national traitor". I simply wish to explain the facts and meaning of his relationship to the Trotskyists, and to say that any attempt to research his life and thought that tries to bypass this relationship is as self-deceiving as the stupid thief who in trying to steal a bell plugs his own ears in the hope that no one will hear it ringing.

There is no way that Chen's membership and leadership of the Chinese Trotskyist organisation can be denied, or of denying that while in gaol he continued through secret channels to control that organisation. There are documents and articles to show that this is true. His declaration after leaving

---

71. A Maoist expression, used in opposition to a "contradiction between the enemy and us [i.e., the revolutionary people]".

gaol that he no longer had dealings with the Trotskyist organisation was mere diplomatic verbiage. At that time he wanted to unite democratic personages beyond the influence of the Guomindang and the Chinese Communist Party in the war against Japan, so he wanted to avoid getting entangled at the outset in the Trotskyist question; in any case, by then the leadership of the Trotskyist organisation had been taken over by Peng Shuzhi, so Chen was not inclined to submit his statements and actions to its disciplinary constraints. But it is clear from contemporary sources that he had by no means left the Chinese Trotskyist organisation. His 1938 letter to Chen Qichang and others, which still exists, is enough to show that he still considered the Trotskyist organisation his own, that he looked upon Luo Shifan, Chen Qichang, Zhao Ji, and Han Jun as his own cadres, and that he criticised them only because he cared for them and for the Trotskyist organisation, even though he was not then working to revive Trotskyist organisation. In early 1939 or late 1938 the Trotskyist organisation sent Chen Qichang by devious routes from Shanghai to Jiangjin to meet Chen Duxiu, and to pass on Trotsky's advice to him to leave the country. Chen wrote a personal letter to Trotsky the tone of which showed quite clearly that he considered the Trotskyist organisation his own: the sharp criticisms he raised in it only showed that he still loved and cherished this body. Let's quote some passages from his letter.

> The membership of the Chinese Communist Party is far in excess of ours, but they're just armed forces with intellectuals but without any working-class base at all. We have fewer than fifty people in Shanghai and Hongkong, plus probably more than one hundred stragglers in other parts of the country.
>
> Needless to say, we do not fool ourselves that we will grow quickly in this war, but if we had pursued more or less right tactics, we would not be in our present feeble state. From the very start our group tended toward ultra-left positions.... A small closed-door ultra-left organisation of this sort obviously stands no chance of winning members; and even if it did, it would be an obstacle to the further development of the Chinese Revolution....
>
> We should beware of perpetuating the illusion that we can only restart our activities after the recovery of territories now occupied by the Japanese. Even today, while Japan continues to occupy parts of our country, we should prepare forthwith to start work afresh, within the narrow space that remains open to us....
>
> If ultra-leftists who stay aloof from the masses and the real struggle ... continue to brag and pretend to be big leaders, to organise leadership bodies that lack all substance, and to found petty kingdoms for themselves behind closed doors and relying on the name of the Fourth International, they will achieve nothing beyond the tarnishing of the Fourth International's prestige in China.

Ask yourself, are those the words of someone who has placed himself outside the Chinese Trotskyist organisation?

At the time of the Hitler-Stalin Pact, Chen Duxiu became so angry that he said things in letters to his friends that went beyond the limit of what is permissible, but it would be wrong to take that as proof that he had broken with Trotskyism.

I have in my possession an article he wrote on May 13, 1942, a fortnight or so before his death. The article, called "The Future of Oppressed Peoples", shows that he remained a Trotskyist to his dying day. Here are some excerpts from it.

> So in my opinion, in a capitalist-imperialist world, no small or weak people can hope for a future so long as it tries only behind closed doors, relying only on its own small forces, to remove the reality of imperialist aggression. Its only hope lies with oppressed toilers the world over. The national question will automatically be resolved if the oppressed, backward peoples unite, overthrow imperialism everywhere, and replace the old world of international capitalism based on commodity deals with a new world of international socialism based on mutual help and a division of labour.

This passage shows that right up to his death Chen Duxiu continued to stand on the side of Trotsky's world revolution and rejected Stalin's idea of socialism in one country.

The article also says:

> Some people vilify the Soviet Union of the early period, whereas we support it; others flatter the Soviet Union of the later period, whereas we detest it. There's a very big difference between these two periods. In the former period the Soviet Union stood for world revolution; in the latter, for Russian national self-interest. Ever since the Soviet leaders first betrayed their own cause after the setback to the revolution in Western Europe and abandoned the policy of putting world revolution to the fore, replacing it instead with Russian national self-interest, clear-thinking people in all countries have gradually progressed from scepticism to disappointment; and though some still think that the hope for mankind lies with the Soviet Union, in reality they can only view it as one among a number of world powers. People who stubbornly insist on calling it socialist only besmirch the name of socialism.

This passage too supports Trotsky and opposes Stalin. The difference is that Trotsky still considered the "Soviet Union of the later period" to be a "degenerated workers' state", whereas Chen Duxiu denounced it point-blank as a one of the "world powers". It's a fact that the "Soviet Union of the later period" had already degenerated into "social-imperialism"; it had started to degenerate from the time of Stalin onwards.

So Chen Duxiu remained a Trotskyist till his dying day, from both an organisational and a theoretical point of view.

Looking back, the main "injustices, frame-ups, and mistakes"[72] were the show-trials of the 1930s, which practically wiped out a generation of revolutionaries. Even today the victims of these trials are treated with contempt. First they must be rehabilitated.

Needless to say, I am speaking not from a juridical point of view. Only a Soviet court, under the control of the Communist Party, can judicially rehabilitate these victims – the so-called "Trotskyites", "Zinovievites", and "Bukharinites". I am speaking only from the point of view of historical fact. From the point of view of history, i.e., from the point of view of the overwhelming majority of knowledgeable people in the world, these victims have long since been rehabilitated. Just a short time ago the new Pope John Paul II rehabilitated Galileo, but for the past several hundred years there can hardly have been anyone still convinced by the charges against Galileo. Today probably only a handful of people in the world still believe the Moscow verdicts against the "Trotskyites".

A footnote in Mao Zedong's *Selected Works* quotes Stalin as follows:

> In the past, seven or eight years ago, Trotskyism was one of such political trends in the working class, an anti-Leninist trend, it is true, and therefore profoundly mistaken, but nevertheless a political trend.... Present-day Trotskyism is not a political trend in the working class, but a gang without principle and without ideas, of wreckers and diversionists, intelligence service agents, spies, murderers, a gang of sworn enemies of the working class, working in the pay of the intelligence services of foreign states.[73]

Stalin said this in 1937, in the period of the Moscow show-trials. But on what grounds did Stalin claim that the Trotskyists were "agents, spies, murderers"? True, Vishkinsky, who was in charge of investigations, came up with all sorts of "criminal evidence", but this "evidence" has already been systematically rebutted by the Dewey Committee. This Committee published two volumes of findings to show that the charges were groundless, and it declared

---

72. A phrase often used in China in the wake of the Cultural Revolution to describe the "fascist lawlessness" of the "Gang of Four".
73. Quoted in Mao Tse-tung, *Selected Works*, Beijing: Foreign Languages Press, 1964, vol. 1, p. 177, fn. 31.

Trotsky innocent. Dewey apart, other evidence has accumulated over the past forty or more years that I would like to mention.

According to Stalin, Trotsky's two biggest crimes were to assassinate Kirov and to spy for the Gestapo in order to help plot Germany's invasion of the Soviet Union.

First the assassination of Kirov. Even at the time, Trotsky came up with evidence to show that Stalin himself killed Kirov to frame the then opposition, but this evidence did not have much impact. More than twenty years later, Stalin's successor Khrushchev, at the Twenty Second Congress of the Communist Party of the Soviet Union, proved that Kirov had indeed been killed by Stalin. Recently twenty letters by Stalin's daughter Svetlana were published in China. In one of them Svetlana denies Khrushchev's allegation and says that Kirov was killed not by Stalin but by Beria. Whatever the case, in today's world, including in the Soviet Union, no one – or at least hardly anyone – any longer believes that Kirov was killed by Zinoviev and Trotsky.

Stalin also killed Tukhachevsky, Blücher, and two other Red Army generals on trumped-up charges of having secret dealings with the Nazis and plotting to betray the Soviet Union. But at the Twenty Second Congress, Khrushchev declared these allegations too to be Stalin's fabrications. Stalin had first forged them and then surreptitiously leaked them to President Benes of Czechoslovakia. Benes, believing them to be true, secretly informed Stalin, who imposed death sentences on the basis of them.

This is just one piece of "evidence" among many. After the Second World War, when the Allies tried the Nazis for war crimes at Nuremberg, some well-known people led by H. G. Wells wrote to the Tribunal asking it to produce from among its vast files evidence of Trotskyist collaboration with the Nazis. It couldn't.

For the time being, I'll restrict myself to just these three points. There is a mountain of evidence to show that the charges levelled against the Trotskyists at the Moscow show trials were groundless, and another mountain of evidence produced by the Dewey Committee. Today researchers can investigate whether or not this evidence substantiates Stalin's charges against the Trotskyists.

As for the Trotskyist organisation in China, there is ample evidence to clear its name. It has already been shown that Chen Duxiu and Luo Han did not act via Tang Youren as paid agents for Japanese intelligence, but the strange thing is that people still believe that the Chinese Trotskyists did. It has been proved that Chen Duxiu was not a Guomindang agent or a running dog of

Chiang Kai-shek, but people still think that the Chinese Trotskyists were. The charges against Chen Duxiu could not stand up under scrutiny. But what is the evidence against the organisation of the Chinese Trotskyists? Can it stand up under scrutiny?

We commemorate Chen Duxiu, this outstanding figure of modern Chinese and world politics. In commemorating him, we Trotskyists are more deeply stirred than other people. We recall that for a while he was General Secretary of our organisation. We consider this an honour.

Appendix 9

PREFACE TO THE COLLECTED POEMS OF CHEN DUXIU[74]

Xiao Ke

In August 1981, speaking at an academic symposium, the veteran Communist General Xiao Ke praised Chen Duxiu's role in the Chinese Revolution and hinted at the possibility of a rehabilitation not only of Chen himself but also of his previously reviled Trotskyist comrades. In his talk, General Xiao Ke also summarised various positive evaluations of Chen Duxiu by Mao Zedong and Zhou Enlai.

❦

Comrades Ren Jianshu, Li Yueshan, and Jin Shupeng have asked me to write a preface to their edition of Chen Duxiu's collected poems, and to write the title of the book in calligraphy. I know little about poetry, but the fact that the collection was by Chen Duxiu excited my interest.

Chen Duxiu was the early twentieth century's man of the hour. When I was young, I read many of his essays in *Duxiu wencun* ("Duxiu's writings"), in bound volumes of *Xin qingnian* ("New youth"), and in *Xiangdao* ("Guide weekly"). But I don't recall reading any of his poems, so I was pleasantly surprised to see this collection. I feel that in this nation where poems and songs are so highly valued, it is essential that Chen's poems are edited and published.

I would like to argue at this point that Chen should be seriously studied. After the defeat of the Great Revolution [of 1925-1927], Chen split from the Party and I no longer trusted him politically, so my impression of him gradually dimmed. But I continued to admire his essays and meritorious exploits in the struggle to resist feudal remnants and superstition and to promote science and democracy. I constantly followed the course of his life and his situation in the years between the defeat of the Great Revolution and his death [in 1942]. On August 18, 1981, at an academic symposium to mark the sixtieth anniversary of the founding of the Chinese Communist Party, I gave a speech a passage of which I shall now quote:

74. Xiao Ke, "Chen Duxiu shiji xu" ("Preface to the collected poems of Chen Duxiu"), in *Xin wenxue shiliao*, no. 1, 1994, pp. 32-33.

In the past, the Chen Duxiu question was taboo; today it is semi-taboo, by which I mean that although today no few people have touched on some aspects of that question, their research is not yet all-sided, nor is it profound. Probably people still have some apprehensions in this regard. Must this question be researched in a comprehensive fashion? My answer is yes. Comrade Mao Zedong said, "Chen Duxiu was the Commander-in-Chief of the May Fourth Movement," Chen Duxiu and Li Dazhao and others "gathered together" progressive youth of that period who had embraced Marxism and "founded the Communist Party..., which was his merit". "When we come to write China's history, we must note his merit in that regard." Comrade Zhou Enlai too said: "Chen Duxiu performed a meritorious service in founding the Communist Party." In my opinion, we should make an all-sided evaluation of this Commander-in-Chief of a glorious age, this distinguished founder of the Party, even though in his later period he committed the error of rightist capitulationism and became a Trotsky-Chen liquidationist after his expulsion from the Party. Comrade Mao Zedong also said, "In various respects, Chen Duxiu resembled Russia's Plekhanov." I completely agree with that assessment; unless we conscientiously research Chen Duxiu, our future writing of Party history could become lop-sided. Not long ago, I watched [the documentary film] *Xianquzhede ge* ("Pioneers' song"), which said nothing about Chen Duxiu, Commander-in-Chief of the May Fourth Movement and the most important figure in the founding of the Party. Only Li Dazhao appears in the lens of this film. But it is a universally recognised fact of history that "Chen in the south and Li in the north" [played the main role in founding the Party]. Although it is true that Li Dazhao was a principal figure in the founding of the Party, the prime place [in that process] belonged to Chen Duxiu. We should not blame the comrades who wrote the script and directed the film for committing this kind of error; it is a problem relevant to research into the history of our Party. In my opinion, in the course of researching Chen Duxiu we cannot confine ourselves merely to his days in the Party or before the founding of the Party, but must also include the Trotsky-Chen liquidationist period. What were the differences between China's Trotsky-Chen liquidationist faction and foreign Trotskyists? How was their programme? What was their attitude to Chiang Kai-shek's Guomindang regime? What was their attitude to the Communist Party? What was their attitude to imperialism and in particular to Japanese imperialism? How did they acquit themselves in the gaols of the Guomindang? What was [Chen's] political attitude between his release from prison [in 1937] and his death? All these issues need to be researched. As for our evaluation of Chen Duxiu, we should follow Comrade Mao Zedong's guidance and learn too from Lenin's critical view and standpoint. From 1903 until the period of the October Revolution [in 1917], Lenin repeatedly criticised Plekhanov's ideological and political errors. Especially during the period of the imperialist [First World] War, he criticised Plekhanov as a "mediocrity", a "social chauvinist", and a "Marxist renegade". But after Plekhanov's death, at a joint conference of the All-Russia Executive of the Central

Committee of Soviets and the Moscow City Soviet with the Trade Unions, he stood together with all the delegates in silent tribute to Plekhanov. Later, a memorial meeting in Leningrad was attended by Lunacharsky and Zinoviev representing the Moscow Party and Government. Not long afterwards, Lenin ordered the publishing of Plekhanov's complete works, established the Plekhanov Institute, and called on everyone to study Plekhanov's philosophy. "Unless we study Plekhanov's entire philosophical writings," he said, "we will never become conscious, true communists." Lenin made a concrete analysis of Plekhanov's political activity and attitudes in each of his various periods. When Stalin at the time of the War of National Defence [i.e., the Second World War] listed the twenty most outstanding people in Russian history, Plekhanov came top of his list. Just because they criticised him, they did not rob him of his position in history, nor in commending his virtues did they conceal his vices. I do not say that we should use the same concrete methods in relation to Chen Duxiu as the Russian Party in relation to Plekhanov. I simply mean that we should approach that problem by adopting Lenin's view and standpoint. (See "Dangshi huiyi baogaoji" ("Reports made at the meeting on Party history"), pp. 39-69.)

In my opinion, in studying Chen Duxiu we should not just confine ourselves to political questions but we should look also at other relevant issues. Comrades Ren, Li, and Jin, in editing Chen Duxiu's collected poems, have provided us with material for such a study. Chen wrote his poems half a century ago.[75] The reader needs to know the age in and the difficulties under which they were conceived, and the process of ideological development that they reflect. "Poetry speaks of lofty ambitions." This statement is true too of the poetry of Chen Duxiu, and is especially evident in the purposefulness of the poetry of his late period, for example the long poem *Jinfenlei* ("Tears alongside luxury and debauchery").[76] The study of Chen Duxiu's poetry helps in the understanding of other aspects of his career.

June 2, 1993

75. We know of 140 poems written by Chen Duxiu over a span of nearly forty years, from 1903 to 1942. Only one of these poems was written in the 1920s, when Chen devoted almost his entire energy to revolutionary activity. He resumed his poetry-writing in the early 1930s, after he had been put in prison. Chen's 140 poems were either published in journals or kept in manuscript by his old friends.
76. This poem, which consists of 56 stanzas, was written in Nanjing Prison in 1934. It satirised the corruption, debauchery, tyranny, and capitulation to the Japanese invaders of the Chiang Kai-shek regime, and expressed deep sympathy for those suffering under that regime. The phrase *liuchao jinfendi* usually denotes Nanjing, which was Chiang Kai-shek's capital, but *jinfen* also means "gold" and "women", i.e., corruption and debauchery.

Glossary

Anhui baihua bao	《安徽白话报》
bagu	八股
beibaohuguo	被保护国
Bo Gu	博古
Bo Liewu	柏烈武
Bo Wenwei	柏文蔚
Cai Jiemin	蔡孑民
Cai Yuanpei	蔡元培
Chen Duxiu	陈独秀
Chen Duxiu yanjiu	《陈独秀研究》
Chen Hanzhang	陈汉章
Chen Jiongming	陈炯明
Chen Qiaonian	陈乔年
Chen Qichang	陈其昌
Chen Yannian	陈延年
Dai Li	戴笠
daotong	道统
De	德

Deng Chanqiu	邓蟾秋
Deng Xiekang	邓燮康
Deng Zhongchun	邓仲纯
Dong Biwu	董必武
Dongxiang	《动向》
Dongxiang yuebao	《动向月报》
Douzheng	《斗争》
Duan Qirui	段祺瑞
Fan Hongyan	范鸿偃
Fuhougang	傅厚岗
Gao Yuhan	高语罕
Gu Hongming	辜鸿铭
Guomin ribao	《国民日报》
Han Jun	寒君
He Haiqiao	何海樵
He Mengxiong	何孟雄
He Zhiyu	何之瑜
He Zishen	何资深
Heshanping	鹤山坪
Hongxian	洪宪
Hu Qiuyuan	胡秋原

Hu Shi	胡适
Hu Zongnan	胡宗南
Huang Kan	黄侃
Huohua	《火花》
Jiangjin	江津
Jin Shupeng	靳树鹏
Jinfenlei	《金粉泪》
jinhua	进化
juren	举人
Kang Sheng	康生
Kang Youwei	康有为
Katayama Sen	片山潜
Li Dazhao	李大钊
Li Furen	李福仁
Li Guangdi	李光地
Li Hongzhang	李鸿章
Li Lisan	李立三
Li Shizeng	李石曾
Li Yueshan	李岳山
Liangen	连根
Liang Qichao	梁启超

Liang Rengong	梁任公
Lin Boqu	林伯渠
Lin Maosheng	林茂生
lingyuan	陵园
Liu Renjing	刘仁静
Liu Ruilong	刘瑞龙
Liu Shuya	刘叔雅
Liu Xiang	刘湘
liuchao jinfendi	六朝金粉地
Lu Xun	鲁迅
Lugaojian	陆稿荐
Luo Han	罗汉
Luo Shifan	罗世藩
Peng Shuzhi	彭述之
Poxiao	《破晓》
Pu Dezhi	濮德志
Pu Qingquan	濮清泉
puxue	朴学
Qian Xuantong	钱玄同
Qin Bangxian	秦邦宪
Qu Qiubai	瞿秋白

Ren Jianshu	任建树
Sai	赛
Shenbao	《申报》
Shi'an zizhuan	《实庵自传》
Shiwu	《时务》
Shizhi	适之
Shouyi	守一
Shuang Shan	双山
Sun Maochi	孙茂池
Tan Sitong	谭嗣同
Tang Baolin	唐宝林
Tang Bin	汤斌
Tang Youren	唐有任
Tao Menghe	陶孟和
Tao Xisheng	陶希圣
Wang Fanxi	王凡西
Wang Jingwei	汪精卫
Wang Mengzou	汪孟邹
Wang Ming	王明
Wang Ruofei	王若飞
Wang Zhaoqun	王兆群

Wen Tianxiang	文天祥
Wu Jiyan	吴季严
Wu Peifu	吴佩孚
Wuchanzhe	《无产者》
Xiangdao	《向导》
Xianquzhede ge	《先驱者的歌》
Xiao Ke	萧克
Xie Wei	谢伟
Xiliu	西流
Xin qingnian	新青年
Xinhua ribao	《新华日报》
xiucai	秀才
Xizhi	希之
Xue Yue	薛岳
Yan Fu	严复
Yang Dusheng	杨笃生
Ye Jianying	叶剑英
Yi Yin	意因
Yin Kuan	尹宽
Yuan Shikai	袁世凯
Yue Fei	岳飞

Zhang Binglin	章炳麟
Zhang Guotao	张国焘
Zhang Junmai	张君劢
Zhang Shizhao	章士钊
Zhang Xingyan	章行严
Zhang Xueliang	张学良
Zhang Yufa	张玉法
Zhang Zhidong	张之洞
Zhang Zigang	张子刚
Zhanggufeng	张鼓峰
Zhao Ji	赵济
Zheng Chaolin	郑超麟
Zheng Xuejia	郑学稼
Zhong Xianchang	钟宪鬯
Zhongfu	仲甫
Zhou Fuling	周弗陵
Zhou Shuren	周树人
Zhou Zuoren	周作人

Index

Bacon, Francis, 137
Belinsky, Vissarion, 141
Benes, President, 148
Bergson, Henri, 123
Beria, Lavrenti P., 148
Blücher, Vasilii K., 148
Bo Gu (Qin Bangxian), 111–112
Bo Liewu (Bo Wenwei), 125–126
Bo Wenwei. See Bo Liewu
Borodin, Mikhail M., 13
Bose, Subhas Chandra, 93
Brüning, Heinrich, 53, 64
Buchman, Alex, vii, 51
Bukharin, Nikolai I., 138
Cai Jiemin. See Cai Yuanpei
Cai Yuanpei (Cai Jiemin), 5, 9, 32,
    116–120
Chamberlain, Neville, 90
Chang, Carsun. See Zhang Junmai
Chen Hanzhang, 117
Chen Qiaonian, 7, 28
Chen Qichang, 12, 31, 29–42, 67, 69,
    112, 145
Chen Yannian, 7, 28
Chernyshevsky, Nikolai G., 141
Chiang Kai-shek, 6–10, 13, 20, 33, 44–
    45, 47–48, 51, 67, 73, 112, 121,
    140, 151–152
Churchill, Winston, 97
Cixi, 117
Clemenceau, Georges, 82
Comte, Auguste, 137
Dai Li, 23

Darwin, Charles, 137
Deng Chanqiu, 121
Deng Xiekang, 121
Deng Zhongchun, 75
Dewey, John, 147
Dickens, Charles, 137
Dong Biwu, 110–111
Duan Qirui, 121
Engels, Friedrich, 51, 56, 74
Eucken, Rudolf, 123
Fan Hongyan, 126
Feigon, Lee, 11, 30, 34
Galileo, 147
Gandhi, Mahatma, 96
Gao Yuhan, 28, 121
Glass, Frank (Li Furen), 42, 49, 114,
    128
Goethe, Johann Wolfgang von, 137
Gu Hongming, 117
Guesde, Jules, 128
Halifax, Viscount, 91
Han Jun, 41–42, 145
He Haiqiao, 116
He Zhiyu (He Zishen), 31–33, 63, 75,
    102, 139
He Zishen. See He Zhiyu
Hegel, Georg Wilhelm Friedrich, 137
Hitler, Adolf, 20–21, 24, 50–54, 57–58,
    60–64, 66, 68, 72–73, 79–81, 88, 90–
    92, 99–100, 146
Hu Qiuyuan, 75–76
Hu Shi (Shizi), 5, 11, 31–32, 44, 77,
    117, 120, 124–125, 135, 137, 140

Hu Zongnan, 23
Huang Kan, 117
Hugo, Victor, 137
Isaacs, Harold, 67
Jin Shupeng, 150, 152
John Paul, Pope, 147
Kagan, Richard, 35
Kang Sheng, 9, 114
Kang Youwei, 3, 117, 134-135
Kant, Immanuel, 137
Katayama Sen, 114
Kautsky, Karl, 22, 76, 98, 133
Kirov, Sergei M., 148
Knox, Frank, 90
Krushchev, Nikita S., 148
Kumarajiva, 124
Kuo, Thomas (Guo Chengtang), 34-35
Lenin, Vladimir I., 11, 50-52, 56, 59-
    60, 65-66, 76-77, 98, 130, 140-141,
    151
Li Dazhao, 5-7, 27, 133, 125, 137,
    143, 151
Li Guangdi, 119
Li Hongzhang, 4, 85
Li Huaying, 111
Li Lisan, 7
Li Shizeng, 15
Li Yueshan, 150, 152
Liang Qichao (Liang Rengong), 117,
    123-124, 134-135
Liang Rengong. See Liang Qichao
Liangen. See Wang Fanxi
Lin Boqu, 109, 111
Lin Maosheng, 34
Litvinov, Maksim M., 90-91
Liu Renjing, 46, 67

Liu Ruilong, 15
Liu Shaoqi, 133
Liu Shipei, 117
Liu Shuya, 126
Liu Xiang, 85
Lloyd George, David, 82
Lu Xun, 9, 135, 143
Lunacharsky, Anatoli V., 14, 152
Luo Han, 41-43, 108-113, 143, 148
Luo Shifan, 40-41, 58, 112, 145
Luther, Martin, 124
Mao Zedong, 7-11, 15, 17-18, 25, 33,
    41, 44, 107, 116, 133, 147, 150-151
Marx, Karl, 11, 50, 56, 73, 98
Mussolini, Benito, 62, 66
Napoleon III, 52-53
Nehru, Jawaharlal, 92-93, 96
Pasteur, Louis, 137
Peng Shuzhi, 16-17, 22, 39, 41-42, 58,
    112, 127
Plekhanov, Georgi V., 19, 22, 128-
    129, 141, 151-152
Pu Dezhi (Xiliu, Pu Qingquan), 31,
    40, 50, 54, 56-58, 60, 62, 107
Pu Qingquan. See Pu Dezhi
Qian Xuantong, 117, 135
Qu Qiubai, 7, 138
Ren Jianshu, 34, 150, 158
Roosevelt, Franklin D., 88, 97
Rousseau, Jean-Jacques, 137
Shachtman, Max, 127
Shizi. See Hu Shi
Shouyi. See Wang Fanxi
Shuang Shan. See Wang Fanxi
Sneevliet, Henk, 12, 19,
Snow, Edgar, 133

Stalin, Joseph V., 8, 12–14, 20–21, 23–24, 47, 50, 53, 59, 61–66, 69, 71–73, 138–140, 146, 148

Stalin, Svetlana, 148

Sun Jiyi, 75–76

Sun Maochi, 121

Sun Xi, 40

Sun Yat-sen, 3–6, 135

Tan Sitong, 3, 117

Tang Baolin, 27, 29, 34

Tang Bin, 119

Tang Youren, 143, 148

Tao Menghe, 75

Tao Xisheng, 32

Trotsky, Leon D., 11–13, 17, 19–20, 25, 27, 31, 44, 49–50, 53, 59, 61, 65–67, 76–77, 108, 114–115, 128–129, 138, 145–146, 148, 151

Tukhachevsky, Mikhail, 148

Vishinsky, Andre, 147

Voitinsky, Grigori, 6, 12, 19

Voroshilov, Kliment Y., 90

Wang Fanxi (Liangen, Shouyi, Ming-yuen Wang, Shuang Shan), ix–x, 11–12, 19–24, 32, 35–36, 54–55, 57–58, 59, 62–64, 69, 114, 127, 130, 133

Wang Guangyuan, 33

Wang Jingwei, 7, 9, 13,

Wang Mengzou, 125

Wang Ming, 7, 9, 17, 27, 112, 114, 139

Wang, Ming-yuen. See Wang Fanxi

Wang Ruofei, 110

Wells, H. G., 148

Wen Tianxiang, 116

Wilde, Oscar, 137

Wilhelm I, 51–52

Wilhelm II, 52

Wilson, Woodrow, 82

Wu Jiyan, 63

Wu Peifu, 85

Xiao Ke, 27, 150

Xie Wei, 29

Xiliu. See Pu Dezhi

Xizhi. See Wu Jiyan

Xue Yue, 45

Yan Fu, 3–4

Yang Dusheng, 116

Ye Jianying, 41, 109–111

Yi Yin. See Zheng Chaolin

Yin Kuan, 42

Yuan Shikai, 4–5, 117, 125–126, 135

Yue Fei, 28

Zhang Binglin, 9, 117

Zhang Guotao, 112

Zhang Jingru, 29

Zhang Junmai (Carsun Chang), 123

Zhang Xingyan, 116

Zhang Xueliang, 9

Zhang Yufa, 34

Zhang Zhidong, 86–8795

Zhang Zigang, 126

Zhao Ji, 40–41, 50, 57, 69, 112, 145

Zheng Chaolin (Yi Yin), 16, 23, 28, 33, 35–36, 39, 42–43, 47, 61–62, 107, 127, 142

Zheng Xuejia, 22, 34, 76

Zhi Yuru (Chih Yu-ju), 34–35

Zhong Xianchang, 116

Zhou Enlai, 54, 133, 150–151

Zhou Fuling, 121

Zhou Zuoren, 135

Zinoviev, Grigori E., 148, 152

Zola, Emile, 137

For Product Safety Concerns and Information please contact our EU
representative GPSR@taylorandfrancis.com
Taylor & Francis Verlag GmbH, Kaufingerstraße 24, 80331 München, Germany

www.ingramcontent.com/pod-product-compliance
Lightning Source LLC
Chambersburg PA
CBHW050713280326
41926CB00088B/3018

9 7 8 1 1 3 8 3 4 3 1 9 1